Drinking Sucks!
Dominate Alcohol, Get Fit, Be Happy

CHRIS SCOTT

ISBN: 0692185674
ISBN-13: 978-0692185674

DEDICATION

To my parents. Without your understanding and encouragement,
none of these epiphanies would have been possible.

TABLE OF CONTENTS

CHAPTER 1

WELCOME TO DRINKING SUCKS!

"The best drug of all is conquering raw reality. Find your vision.
Own it. Never give up. You'll forget the artificial highs even existed."
-Chris Scott

Unlike many people who try to live one day at a time without booze, I've come to believe that drinking sucks.

If you've ever struggled with a drinking problem, this belief can be lifesaving. It is not, however, something that you can simply will yourself to believe. In my case, it resulted from a lot of personal work and independent research that I've condensed for you in this book.

If your reaction to the title of this book is: "Drinking doesn't suck, it's the best thing ever!" then I will lend you a different perspective. If your first thought instead is, "Drinking sucks - compared to what?" then rest assured that I will answer your question.

Everyone knows that it's hard for alcoholics to quit drinking. The deeper truth is that heavy drinkers - people who get wasted on a regular basis, and who are the least likely to describe themselves as addicted - have no idea what they're missing out on.

I will illuminate the vast possibility of life beyond alcohol. And I will share with you the blueprint, which is really a METHOD and a MINDSET combined into a LIFESTYLE, that makes a natural aversion to drinking possible.

But because knowledge is potential power, first we will explore the nature of alcohol addiction in detail. I will tell you about supplements that can help you tremendously if you're dependent on alcohol. If you have a problem that is beginning to spiral out of control, you can save yourself a lot of misery down the road by using the methods in this book.

I also want to clarify that I've come to believe that drinking sucks despite the fact that nearly everyone I know still drinks. They don't suck. They can, and often do, drink in front of me. My view of them and of drinking remain the same: they're great; drinking sucks. I neither pity them nor feel jealous of them. My opinion of drinking is a personal one that doesn't affect my relationships. With that said, I choose not to hang around people who drink daily or heavily.

My own story will serve as the backdrop for my broader message. As I approach another birthday with a zero in it, I see that my conviction that drinking sucks saved my life. I didn't believe it when I quit drinking, but the epiphany gradually bubbled to the surface of my conscious mind, reinforcing everything else I did to transcend drinking culture and take charge of my life.

Soon you will see that life without alcohol is NOT a life of deprivation. You will see that heavy drinkers, alcoholics or not, are the ones who are the most deprived. You will gain a new arsenal of tools to help you get more out of your life. And since you will have more ideas about how to live life to the fullest without missing out on anything and without succumbing to drinking culture, you will find it easier to feel grateful for your present and optimistic about your future.

If you don't have a drinking problem, you can still take away a lot from this book. You will have a better grasp of alcohol addiction and how to help loved ones who are suffering from this condition. You might also find a few reasons to cut down on booze yourself.

Drinking sucks more out of people than people suck out of drinking, even if most of them (including the great Winston Churchill) never realize it.

The purpose of this book is NOT to simply list the myriad ways in which alcohol can ruin your life. Cirrhosis patients in hospitals and local drunks on street corners can list these ways better than I can.

Chances are good that you have plenty of your own evidence that drinking sucks. And yet the evidence provided by your own senses directly conflicts with the attitudes of your friends, and with the barrage of persuasion tactics you've absorbed over the years from clever alcohol manufacturers.

Another way out of alcohol addiction is possible; one that doesn't have to involve meetings, repeating dogma, or taking antidepressants. I don't judge anyone who participates in these things. At one point, I figured I might have to participate in all of them. I'm glad that I was wrong.

While I have strong views, I also have a strong aversion to dogma. I'll state now that anything I write could be wrong. I'm convinced that it's 100% true, but it's all rooted in my experience, and you can decide which ideas to keep or discard.

Don't believe anything I write without trying anything for yourself. On the flip side, please don't dismiss anything out of hand.

Contrary to conventional wisdom, your best friend in dominating alcohol addiction is a free spirited and open sense of life; perhaps even a healthy fear of missing out on life. Most people who quit drinking channel this fear into missing alcohol. When they were drinking, and now that they're sitting in chairs and missing drinking, their constant, unfortunate truth is that they've been missing out on life all along. In the past, they focused on a poison - and now they're focusing on the absence of that poison.

My hallmark trait has always been the kind of obsessive curiosity that addiction counselors warn against. I see in retrospect that it saved me, because it drove me to rebuild my physiology and my mind so that I could start feeling like the man I was born to be. These days,

I want to lift heavy weights and I want to learn everything I can about the vast, mystifying, rapidly changing world around me.

Natural endorphins are my drugs of choice and an unquenchable thirst for knowledge is my motivation for getting up every morning.

My life has improved since I was drinking nearly a handle of vodka in front of the TV on a Tuesday night, passing out on my couch, and then sweating and shaking while trying to button my shirt before another miserable day at work. Before I learned about visualization, I used to visualize everyone glaring at me while I walked into the office, covered in sweat and tensing up to conceal my alcohol withdrawal chills, 15 minutes late. This scene, complete with the dreadful visualization that always came true, probably happened to me several hundred times.

A ruthless commitment to self-improvement was my first rule in dominating alcohol. You don't have to feel like a superhero on Day One to make this commitment. You just have to feel the tiniest of fires burning within you. Even a single spark will do. It's the smoldering desire to grasp toward something, anything, even if it's amorphous and blurry. What you desire is your own resurrection.

The WILL to self-actualize, regardless of what you want to become or when you think you need to become it, can save your life.

If you're in dire straits like I was, then you won't make the leap to total self-actualization from your current situation. This book will proceed methodically, beginning with a workable yet nuanced understanding of addiction, and then moving on to the processes of repairing your brain cells, changing your diet to support your energy levels, and rebuilding your body (and pride) through fitness.

You'll see that dominating alcohol has little to do with luck or willpower. Biochemical repair must precede mental re-conditioning. In other words, you have to rebuild your brain and body before you can control your mind. I make a distinction between the brain and the mind. Your brain is a tangible organ; your mind is the facilitator of your intangible thoughts, feelings, and experiences.

With your physical body healing, we will next discuss how to establish mutually-reinforcing habits - which I call virtuous cycles - and how to reframe your mental concept of alcohol so that you can see it as the worthless toxin that it really is. I'll share tried and true strategies for feeling high on life most of the time. Whether you decide to call yourself "sober" or not is none of my business, but I promise that you can make life your drug of choice. It's all good if you don't believe me yet.

Finally, we'll move on to the subjects of your life's purpose and tribal affiliations, both which are notably absent from every professional discussion of addiction I've ever seen. You won't automatically self-actualize if you stay away from alcohol, and the failure to improve self-image often leads people right back to the bottle.

Your purpose in life does not have to revolve around addiction. Your tribal identity does not need to come from a group of chronically-relapsing "sober friends." These treatment center assumptions, which are meant to shelter recovering people from reality, are actually so limiting and uninspiring that they often become additional obstacles to overcoming addiction.

Growing spiritually and learning how to be a good person are important, but they are not the same things as self-improvement. Like they say in airplanes, you have to figure out how to put your own mask on before you try to help others. Building yourself up so that you can surround yourself with quality people - rather than perpetually hanging around relapsers with their own gravitational pull - is an important part of leaving addiction in the past.

There's a lot of literature on humility, surrender, powerlessness, and other inherently depressing topics. The sentiment is not always wrong, but I would be doing you a disservice if I started repeating recovery cliches. I will focus instead on positive lifestyle strategies that will help you revitalize your sense of life.

Dominating alcohol is like solving a complex puzzle. Most people who have relapsed over and over again are missing big pieces. This book will outline the biggest pieces that are ignored by most addiction specialists - from the perspective of someone who has used copious trial and error, and followed all of his advice before writing it down.

For people who adopt the permanent recovery mindset, alcohol still tends to hold some allure. For people who are recovered, it's a totally moot substance. If you've picked up this book because you've been "sober" for years and yet you still secretly miss alcohol, you can get as much out of it as someone who is brand new to the idea of quitting drinking. Perhaps you are still brand new to the idea that DRINKING SUCKS.

It took me a long time to gather every missing piece of the addiction puzzle and figure out the most common missing pieces. My puzzle is not necessarily the same as yours. But we're probably not all that different. I've written this book to arm you with knowledge that will help you to become recovered in a much shorter period of time than I did.

You'll notice that I have a particular obsession with fitness. Perhaps you prefer painting or fishing, and that's fine with me. Dominating alcohol will require you to find an activity that prevents you from focusing on a negative, especially during your first few months.

But exercise is the most underrated solution for people who want to really dominate alcohol addiction. It's the fastest way to rewire your brain. Regular exercise replenishes your system with oxygen and vital nutrients, releases hormones that create a sense of well-being, and cures anxiety, depression, and insomnia so effectively that many doctors have begun to prescribe it for these conditions instead of medications.

Everyone would take exercise if it were a pill that could be popped. There is a secret, which we will address: the mental block involved in getting your ass to the gym can be dissolved by fixing your nutritional deficiencies first.

If you're thinking, "I drink every night and I work out every day!" - I understand you, I used to do this too. Trust me when I say that the benefits of exercise can't be fully appreciated until after you excise alcohol from your life. You will find that you can get the same feeling from a great workout that you once pursued from alcohol, with none of the negative side effects.

Drinking sucks, but so do bromides about "sobriety" that are posted and reposted on social media accounts by people who can't seem to give up the habit of either drinking or posting about sobriety. My goal is to enable you to transcend the vicious cycle of drinking and quitting and drinking again. I don't want to become a guru. I'm propelled by a sense of mission to write this book, and then to move on to my next project with renewed personal vigor. I hope that I can help you do the same after reading it.

As you finish each chapter, you will subconsciously develop a better grasp of why drinking sucks - and that's a huge piece of the puzzle. I feel sympathy for people who try to stay away from alcohol for years, without ever reversing the years of false conditioning they received about alcohol.

Recognizing that drinking is an unnecessary and time-wasting activity with insane health risks, and that it starts to suck way more quickly for some people than for others, is just one step on the way to realizing your full potential in life. When you repair your brain, rebuild your body, and enjoy total mastery over your mind, you will experience exactly what I am trying to share with you. Ideas that may seem esoteric, even foreign, to you now will make intuitive sense later on.

You might wonder how I came up with the name of this book. My two best college buddies and I live in three different cities, and yet I still get texts from them occasionally saying, effectively, "Oh my God. I shouldn't have gone out last night. Drinking sucks!" Neither of them drink often - they are what we call social drinkers - but they seem to remember when they do that drinking doesn't treat their bodies well. The Millennial Generation drinks half of all the wine in America and 25% of us use alcohol to cope with stress, even though 95% of us "deeply value" our health. This book is primarily about alcohol addiction, but it doesn't take a genius (or an alcoholic) to realize that drinking is a dumb way to deal with stress.

If you think about it, most people know on some level that drinking sucks. People who teetotal or rarely drink understand that drinking isn't all it's cracked up to be, because if they thought otherwise, they would drink more. People who drink every weekend realize that it sucks every weekend morning when their bodies take a beating. The only people who don't know that it sucks are the ones who drink every night and haven't ruined their lives yet, and if they survive long enough to become severe alcoholics, they curiously tend to conclude that they suck.

When I drank every night, I actually saved studies on my laptop about the health benefits of wine - studies funded by alcohol companies - just to feed my illusions. Newer research has found that even light drinking can cause seven types of cancer; the relationship between alcohol and cancer is essentially linear.

What about people who have a passion for drinking and feel great because they always drink in moderation? I know a lot of people who would claim to fit into this category, but I don't know anyone who actually does. In fact, I don't know anyone who feels passionate about something and then decides to do it in moderation. The best part about quitting drinking is being free to live your passions - or pursue your obsessions - with a sense of congruence that comes from knowing that the things you love most are building you up, not tearing you down.

But isn't it impractical to be a nondrinker in our society? Not at all. For people like us, it's way more practical than the alternative. Of course, it's no fun trying to run around explaining this to people.

If someone asks me, "Why don't you drink - are you an alcoholic?" I'll say: "I'm a nondrinker." If I'm alone with the person and I feel like elaborating, I'll say: "I don't do anything I like in moderation." If for some reason the questioner deserves to know about my past, I'll say: "I used to have an alcohol addiction." If they respond, "Oh, so you're an alcoholic," I'll say: "An alcoholic has a drinking problem. I don't drink and I don't want to drink."

"So you're sober?"
"No, I'm perilously high on life."
"Wouldn't you be higher if you had a drink?"
"My feel-good chemicals are already maxed out."
"Well I'm drinking, so you should drink."
"Nah, drinking sucks."

I confess that I enjoy toying with people. But telling weighty personal stories is never the way to go at social events.

My typical response at an event when someone asks, "Why aren't you drinking?" is: "I'm far too young." This reliably gets a laugh and prevents further questioning, since it's obvious that I'm intentionally ignoring the question without sacrificing my sense of humor. I'll give you one more subtle but equally effective response: "I've had enough."

My point is this: If you want to be a nondrinker in our society, you have to own the frames through which you perceive your life.

When I say that drinking sucks, I'm not making a moral argument about drinkers. I also happen to think that raw cauliflower sucks. Few people would question that I reserve the right as a sovereign individual to dislike raw cauliflower. That some people freak out when we say that drinking sucks says more about them (and alcohol's subtle addictive power) than it does about us - which is even further proof that drinking sucks. With that said, I don't preach about my private aversions.

And of course, raw cauliflower has never poisoned my body. Drinking sucks in general, but alcohol addiction is no joke. The next chapter will investigate the nature of alcohol addiction, and you can gain insight from it even if you don't think you are addicted to alcohol.

You can agree or disagree with my approach in this book. Unlike the average self-help book, this one contains a large amount of information. The 30 Day Plan will summarize the main takeaways, but it will not make sense unless you read the chapters sequentially. My hope is that you take away at least a few ideas that change your life for the better.

I'm an adopted survivor of alcohol addiction. I do not know if I have any biological siblings, but this is the book I would write for them if I knew they were out there facing the same struggle that I overcame.

Rehab costs tens of thousands of dollars. Many support groups are free. The whole-body epiphany when you realize that DRINKING SUCKS is priceless.

CHAPTER 2

UNDERSTAND ALCOHOL ADDICTION

"The sole fact that a condition is accompanied by abnormal behavior
does not justify its classification as mental."
-Judge Lord, Granville House v. HHS

When I was 25 years old, I decided to see a psychotherapist for the first time in my life. I lived in a beautiful apartment in New York City, I had great friends, and I made plenty of money. But I had a serious puzzle on my hands: On nights that I DIDN'T drink, I felt physically sick and twitched in my bed all night long without sleeping. The next day felt like a disorienting nightmare until I had a drink.

Friends and family told me a fact of the universe that apparently didn't apply to me: "You know, you don't need alcohol to have fun." This statement always confused me immensely. Who said anything about having fun? Whether anyone was there or not, I needed alcohol to feel like the universe was an acceptable habitat. Fun only came when I tripled or quadrupled my normal intake, which was already enough to kill the average nondrinker.

And so I found a psychotherapist with some of the best reviews in all of New York City. After work one day I went to his office inside of a quaint brick building, stopping first at a bar to calm my nerves with a few glasses of wine. I did not need to feel great, but I needed to be able to think and speak clearly so that he could solve my problem.

A man who looked a lot like Sigmund Freud opened the door and smiled. "Hi there. I'll be glad to help you with your problem. I only accept cash, though." I went to the ATM next door and withdrew $340 in $20 bills and put the wad of cash into his hand.

Not an Emotional Puzzle

I told this man about my problem and he listened sympathetically. I said that I wanted to figure out why I drank. I reasoned that if I could identify the emotion that drove me to drink so much - the root cause of my behavior - I could control my state of mind and start to drink like normal people. I was so addicted to alcohol that the thought of quitting never even occurred to me.

His response caught me off guard: "I'll tell you why you drink. You drink because you have a physical addiction to alcohol. First, we'll need to get you off of alcohol. After that, I'll need you in here five times per week. I'll reduce the rate to $250 for you."

I told him that I didn't have $5,000 per month to spend on this kind of treatment. He recommended AA as the next best thing, and ended the session with a warning: "If you don't get a hold of this problem now, things will get very bad."

As I eventually discovered, he was absolutely right about that. He was also correct in identifying alcohol addiction as a physical problem, rather than an emotional issue.

If you drink too much and you've failed to stop, save yourself $340. Consider the idea that your brain chemistry will not allow you to drink normally. Emotional baggage causes many people to pick up a drink, but it does not cause alcohol addiction.

If I could go back in time, I would explain to myself: *Listen Chris, if you go searching for an emotional root cause for why you metabolize alcohol the way you do - for why your tolerance is so much higher than everyone else's, and for why you have such disastrous withdrawal symptoms when you don't drink for a few days - you'll never find it, because it doesn't exist.*

Not a Social Puzzle

I've heard people try to explain addiction as a social phenomenon. The theory is that some people feel left out of society, and so they get hooked on alcohol or drugs as a replacement for social acceptance.

I'm sure many people drink because they're lonely. My region of the country just went through a major hurricane, and many people I know relocated and drank for five days straight. The vast majority of these people will never be addicted to alcohol.

Yet most of us didn't start our addictions in a social vacuum. I'm still very close to the extraordinary friends I made in high school and college. My friends have never been mere drinking buddies. They were always social drinkers who binged when it was appropriate and watched with confusion as I put down tremendous quantities of alcohol with little noticeable effect.

Studies from the social angle usually go something like this: "Rats who were introduced to playmates immediately started choosing water over alcohol." I'm happy for those rats, but I have nothing in common with them. I have the same great friends today that I had when I was drinking, and for nearly a decade, I rarely chose water over alcohol.

A year before I quit drinking, I actually forced myself to drink water instead of alcohol for a few nights. I shook like I had hypothermia and felt like I was going to die. I chose alcohol after that experiment and felt much better. Of course, the time eventually came when the amount of alcohol I needed to function normally started to make me almost as ill as abstaining from alcohol completely.

The social explanation for addiction cannot properly account for the existence of withdrawal, which some people will never experience no matter how often they drink. It also smacks of the academic obsession with recasting biological realities as social constructs.

Not a Spiritual Puzzle

Conventional wisdom tells us that the root cause of alcohol addiction is less important than the idea that all alcoholics follow a predictable path to self-destruction. As a result, group therapy and spiritual guidance are the most common treatments for alcohol addiction.

Unfortunately, the average AA meeting consists of people who are earnestly working on their spiritual health while ignoring their physical health. Without stabilizing your body, spiritual change can be excruciatingly difficult or even impossible. In AA's defense, many of its participants recognize that alcohol addiction is a "family disease;" a physical problem that can be genetically inherited.

Bill Wilson, one of AA's founders, used Vitamin B3 and even LSD in his efforts to rewire his own brain and leave alcohol addiction in the past. Most treatment centers today use B-Vitamins to help alcoholics replenish their energy levels. In case you thought Bill was a loony for promoting LSD use, consider that a 2014 University of New Mexico study found that psilocybin (in psychedelic mushrooms) can reduce alcohol consumption by 50%. Other studies have found that ibogaine, another psychedelic mushroom compound, can help severe opiate addicts quit spontaneously and without any other treatment.

As the field of neuroscience progresses, it's becoming increasingly clear that addiction stems from malfunctions in our brain circuitry. Our minds can be of enormous assistance in rewiring our brains, but as we will see, adopting a mindset of powerlessness might not be the best way to do this.

But I digress. I'll share with you my biggest objection to the spiritual defect theory. When we classify alcohol addiction as a spiritual problem, we forego the opportunity to help people who have a physical addiction to alcohol that may kill them before it destroys their spiritual epicenters - namely, their relationships and employment. I once fell into this category and I'm lucky to be alive. I know of others who weren't so lucky.

It's not necessary to "hit bottom" before you get help. But let's be serious: If you haven't hit bottom, will you really have any desire to go to AA meetings and listen to biochemically depressed (i.e., withdrawing) people talk about how they ruined their lives? Of course you won't, because you're not there yet and you can't relate.

The solution is not to wait until you can relate. It's to understand the nature of the problem now, and to choose freedom and fulfillment over temporary toxic bliss that can lead you straight to hell on earth.

It's important to resolve emotional problems, foster a healthy social life, and work on spiritual development. But many social drinkers have problems in these areas of life and can't imagine having to drink every day just to feel normal. Something else is at work here.

Alcohol Addiction is a Biochemical Puzzle

All of the evidence I have seen, including my own experience, leads me to believe that the physiologies of people with ACTIVE alcohol addictions are biochemically different from those who do not experience alcohol addiction. They are usually different from the outset, and they become even more different over time because of changes in the brain and body wrought by alcohol.

Here's the tricky part. Alcohol is an addictive drug, period. But certain people are predisposed to becoming dependent on it in a very short period of time. They do NOT have attitude problems or spiritual defects - they have biochemistries that propel them into the vice-like grip of addiction.

By my second year of drinking, I had journal entries that looked like this: "Drink less than 10 drinks at at time. HAVE THREE DAYS PER WEEK WITH NO ALCOHOL." I used the journal only to track my goals. While I exceeded my athletic and academic goals, I never met any of the goals I set for myself in the alcohol category.

How many 19 year olds have an "alcohol" category in their goal journals?

Some people who try everything they can find to "control" their drinking fail to avoid addiction. Yet some people who binge never become addicted to alcohol no matter how hard they seem to test fate.

What accounts for this discrepancy?

For most people, alcohol releases endorphins and is excreted from the body in the form of water and acetic acid. The primary effect of overconsumption is sedation, and too much alcohol results in a hangover. In contrast to powerful opiates like heroin, which can make almost anyone dependent in a short period of time, it takes years of hard drinking for most people to disrupt their brain chemistry enough to become dependent on alcohol. These people are certainly not immune to addiction, but their descent is much slower.

For some of us, by contrast, alcohol presents itself as the most beautiful Trojan horse we've ever seen. Our first drinking experiences tend to stand out like religious epiphanies. Drinking activates invisible biochemical processes that change our lives immediately and move us quickly, although still imperceptibly, toward total dependence.

The first time I drank with friends late at night in high school, I put down close to an entire bottle of 99 Bananas. They laughed at me, then got bored of me, and then went to bed. I absolutely hated the taste, so why did I keep nursing it while they slept? I was chasing a physical sensation unlike anything I had ever experienced in my life. I had no pain or emotional issues to escape from, nor did I have any reason to drink more to seem cool while my friends were sleeping. I just felt like I had finally found heaven on earth. I knew very early on that my "taste" for alcohol had nothing to do with taste at all - and nothing to do with fitting in. It had nothing to do with anyone or anything except the inside of my own brain.

The root causes of alcohol addiction can be complex and even layered. Some people might find it physically impossible to become addicted to alcohol (or anything else). Others might have no genetic predisposition, and yet alter their brains enough over the course of a few hundred parties to become dependent. Genes that affect neurotransmitter balance, liver enzymes that metabolize alcohol, and neurological reward centers can conspire together to make it nearly impossible for some people to stop drinking once they have started. I suspect that the puzzle is not exactly the same for any two people, even if their symptoms are nearly identical.

What matters most is that in progressing toward alcohol dependence, you radically altered your brain's natural equilibrium and the structure of your neural pathways. Over time, alcohol hijacked your entire brain and created a new equilibrium for your brain chemistry.

A number of underlying disorders can increase the severity of alcohol addiction. Prenatal alcohol exposure, post-traumatic stress disorder, and unresolved anxiety and depression are all non-genetic "environmental factors" that can add fuel to the fire. Hypoglycemia, certain food allergies, and pyroluria (a blood chemical disorder) are found in high percentages of people with alcohol addictions. If left untreated, they can make bad cravings for alcohol much more hellish.

The good news is that many of these underlying conditions can be treated successfully through supplementation, diet and exercise. If alcohol made your mood "normal" for the first time in your life, let me assure you that the supplements I recommend can help you feel better without alcohol than you ever imagined.

There are a few more issues I want to illuminate before outlining the solution to the problem...

The Role of Neurotransmitters

No one likes to reduce their experience to scientific terms like neurotransmitters. They seem to belittle and obscure the intensity of our emotions. But think of the most exciting moment of your life. I'm sure it was objectively awesome, but your experience of it as such depended entirely on your brain's ability to supply neurotransmitters in response to it.

Ethanol mimics GABA, a calming neurotransmitter, and inhibits its production over time. It releases dopamine - a chemical associated with problem solving, memory, and craving - causing us to "learn" to drink alcohol in the same way that we once learned to drink water. (Alcohol cravings can become more deeply embedded than cravings for water and food, causing alcoholics to drink themselves to death.) Ethanol suppresses glutamate, a stress chemical, which can rebound and cause feelings of panic a few hours after drinking sessions end.

Severe alcoholics who try to quit alcohol cold turkey experience hell because alcohol becomes a chemical precondition for their progressively deteriorating brain balance. The cruelty of alcohol addiction lies in the fact that it depletes neurotransmitters over time. An alcoholic's baseline level of well-being is always in decline.

A severe alcoholic doesn't drink because he selfishly wants to feel better than everyone else. At one point, 10 drinks might have brought his mood level from good to excellent. Eventually, 30 drinks will bring him from severely depressed to mildly depressed. He still perceives this as a big improvement, but because he craves alcohol as much as water and food, he will not realize that alcohol is the reason he became depressed in the first place. When he tries to abstain, he may sweat and feel suicidal and have nightmares. A few months earlier, his only symptoms might have been a mild sense of unease. Alcohol addiction is a vicious, physical, circular trap that usually worsens over time.

The Role of Endorphins

Endorphins are neurotransmitters that serve as the brain's natural opiates. Everyone releases endorphins in response to alcohol. Our brains associate alcohol with pleasure because it releases endorphins every time we drink.

Yes, drinking is a learned behavior. But for people who are addicted to alcohol, drinking is not a choice in the way that ordering fish instead of steak is a choice. It is a choice in the way that eating or not is a choice, or drinking water or not is a choice. In other words, eating and drinking water are learned behaviors as well. We learned them much earlier in life, although the alcoholic brain assigns a higher priority to alcohol than food or water.

Why would our brains do this? Because it is absorbed through the stomach lining, alcohol sells itself to our brains - and to our autonomic survival mechanisms, over which we have no control - as a quicker and more reliable source of fuel and temporary chemical balance than food.

Back to endorphins. Scientists have long speculated that we might be able to de-fuse the biochemical pathways associated with alcohol addiction if we could manipulate endorphin levels. Over the past decade, this hypothesis has been validated.

The Sinclair Method is a treatment for alcohol addiction that involves taking Naltrexone, an opiate blocker, an hour before drinking. It simply blocks endorphins in the brain. There is no spiritual guidance or any instruction to cut down on drinking. Used over the course of several months, this method produces an 80% success rate in reducing alcohol intake to negligible levels. Since drinking tapers gradually, other brain chemicals do not spike and crash. Withdrawal do not occur. The majority of people who try this method decide to quit for good.

I took Naltrexone for three months after I detoxed off of alcohol. The same doctor who prescribed benzodiazepines for my detox offered it to me, but he did not mention The Sinclair Method. Studies show that taking Naltrexone to support abstinence does not improve relapse statistics. Alcohol has to be consumed in order for the compulsion to drink to be "pharmacologically extinguished." In retrospect, it's clear to me that this doctor was trying to help. He probably figured that I would be among the 90% who relapsed, and that The Sinclair Method would silently work for me. My guess is that because it challenges prevailing spiritual recovery models, he didn't want to name it or explain it.

I still have Naltrexone in my medicine cabinet. It's a last resort in case terrorists contaminate my water supply with ethanol or someone forces me to drink at gunpoint. I have no need to extinguish a compulsion that I've already defeated, though. I don't want to block all of the endorphins that I've figured out how to produce naturally!

A Progressive Condition

Alcohol addiction creates neural pathways that become more entrenched with each drinking session. As these pathways expand, the brain becomes increasingly dependent on alcohol for endorphin release and neurotransmitter balance. Tolerance level and the severity of withdrawal increase over time. If you're addicted to alcohol and you've not yet experienced withdrawal, consider yourself lucky. Get out of the game before it gets really bad.

The phenomenon of brain chemistry by which withdrawal become progressively worse is called kindling. My withdrawal symptoms went from mildly shaky hands to demonic hallucinations and convulsions within the span of about a year.

Why can't we simply stop drinking when we're in the throes of withdrawal? Our limbic systems take over when we reach a certain threshold of suffering. Alcohol has made itself indispensable to our functioning, hijacking our subconscious minds and making itself necessary for our survival. Never doubt the strength of your brain's survival mechanisms. Telling an actively drinking alcoholic to quit drinking immediately will cause the same kind of panic that you might expect from telling a normal person to dehydrate himself to death voluntarily. If it hasn't gotten quite that bad yet, it probably will.

This is the process that AA participants are referring to when they mystically say, "I lost my power of choice." It is a scary thing with a scientific explanation.

The Spectrum of Alcohol Addiction

There are people who appear to have unhealthy relationships with alcohol, yet who do not conform to a pattern of insane daily drinking.

I know older people who are unable to quit drinking despite repeated efforts to stop - and yet who only have a few drinks per day. I know middle aged people who are unable to stop drinking once they start, but who only drink once every few months. Perhaps these people have psychological reasons for preferring to drink the way they do. Or perhaps they are stuck, for now, using willpower to maintain a low-level addiction. Even if it does not spiral out of control in the long-run, it can chip away at their health and lead to costly mistakes.

If you think you might have a predisposition, there's no need to keep rolling the dice. Drinking sucks, regardless of how far down the slippery slope you've gotten.

"Is Alcoholism a Disease?"

Alcohol addiction was classified as a disease by the American Medical Association in 1957. People who argued that it was an attitude problem were clearly wrong. Alcohol addiction is a physical condition, not a mental problem.

If you're going through severe withdrawal, you're more ill than the average hospital patient with a serious disease. You might even die if you don't get help. But if you haven't touched alcohol in 30 years and you genuinely feel that drinking sucks, it makes no sense to treat you like you have a disease. There are various shades of gray in between these two states of existence. Because I have recovered, I do not call myself an alcoholic and I do not say that I have a disease.

Some of the words that we use as a result of classifying alcohol addiction as a disease are problematic. For starters, the word "alcoholism" conjures in my mind a radical religion or ideology obsessed with drinking alcohol. The word is so intensely stigmatized that it overshadows any other qualities of the people it describes.

I refer to people as alcoholics only if they are addicted to alcohol AND still actively drinking, since it's the most commonly understood label for someone suffering from alcohol addiction.

But since people who don't drink cannot be said to have a drinking problem, it makes little sense to refer to longtime nondrinkers as alcoholics. I'd bet that I could reactivate some really bad biochemical processes if I decided to binge for a week straight, but ethanol is about as appealing to me as gasoline or paint thinner. I will explain as the book progresses why this is the case.

During the brief period of time that I attended AA meetings, I got tired of hearing macho dudes say, "My disease is outside doing pushups!" If you envision alcohol as a Super Jacked Disease Villain who's out to get you, then good luck, buddy. Perceptions can become self-fulfilling prophecies. You should be the one outside doing pushups, not your so-called disease. It's unwise to invent a bogeyman and then give him unlimited power.

Diseases like cancer and AIDS restrict people's freedom to live normal lives (or to live at all) regardless of what they do. If you've had an alcohol addiction, there is only one restriction: you can't reasonably expect to drink in moderation, unless you decide to take Naltrexone or some other cutting-edge biochemical treatment. You're in the clear as long as you avoid a very specific substance. As we will see, being a nondrinker can be a painful ordeal or a non-issue, depending largely on your own thoughts and actions. Drinking is a social norm, not an existential necessity, despite the delusions of people with active addictions (myself once included).

Would you call yourself permanently diseased if you discovered that you don't react well to any other compound? Why have we singled out ethanol in this way?

The idea that good health has anything to do with moderating an addictive poison - and that you have a disease if you've failed to moderate it in the past - says more about alcohol's tight grip on our society than it does about you or me.

Is Moderation Possible?

At an AA meeting long ago, I met several old men who were somehow new to that program after struggling with addiction for their whole lives. I don't know how they ultimately fared there, but the fact that they had spent decades trying to drink moderately and jumping from one solution to another before finally ending up at the most common program of all struck me as proof that some people just can't moderate their alcohol intake. At that time, I didn't know anything I've written in this book, and I hadn't even come to believe that drinking sucks. I entertained the idea of drinking again, in moderation of course, sometime in the far future. But I did pause to consider the plight of the old men who had wasted their entire lives chasing moderation.

There is a scientific explanation for what these guys went through. If you have a biochemical predisposition to alcohol addiction, then alcohol will tend to activate addictive behavior, sooner or later. If you have no such predisposition and you became addicted over time, your addiction may have altered your brain permanently, in such a way as to make alcohol an activating factor for that kind of behavior anytime you decide to drink in the future. Simply put, moderation is probably not in the cards if you have experienced alcohol dependence.

The silver lining, as far as I can tell, is that scientific advancements - for example, stem cell injections - may well solve the alcohol addiction problem for good in our lifetimes. (So why not wait until then to worry about the moderation question?) I can assure you that as you rewire your brain, the thought of testing the waters will become less appealing. Over time, it will simply stop occurring to you. Your brain today is not firing the same impulses as it will 6 months, 12 months, or 24 months after you quit drinking. If you implement the information in this book, you will not need to worry about lifelong alcohol cravings.

You might recall a time, long ago, when a single shot gave you a nice buzz. We tend to take this as evidence that we didn't used to have a problem, and we deduce that we can return to this state if we're more responsible. Willpower and responsibility have nothing to do with it. If you've struggled with alcohol addiction at a young age, chances are good that you have an underlying predisposition that was deeply rooted in your cells before you ever drank. Even if you were not predisposed and you altered your brain enough to become addicted, it's very likely that you changed your brain permanently. Biochemistry is not a defect or a curse; it just is. Nature presents us with biological realities and it's up to us to attach a meaning or significance to them.

It's up to you to determine whether you had a situational drinking problem - for example, a few weeks of heavy drinking after the death of someone you loved - or the biochemical disorder known as alcoholism. Some people can binge drink for weeks and emerge without withdrawal or cravings. They may increase their tolerance and even fall down a slippery slope, but their descent is gradual and can last a lifetime. And then there are people like me, who are on the extreme other side of the spectrum. I know for a fact that if I were to drink heavily for a few nights in a row, I would wake up one morning with a festering itch for more and more and more (and more) alcohol. It's happened too many times in the past, after prolonged breaks even, for me to deny that this kind of "behavior" is deeply rooted in my cells. The last thing I want to do is rekindle my past addiction to alcohol.

Willpower and therapy are very unlikely to help you drink moderately. Perhaps you will be able to keep drinking if you opt for The Sinclair Method or some other new treatment that addresses the biochemistry of addiction. I don't judge anyone who chooses a different path than I did. I'll just say that I feel so much better without alcohol - which is a worthless toxin, whether you medicate away its effects or not - that I no longer fantasize about going back to the bottle.

It would be a tall order for scientists to invent a pill that preserves alcohol's temporary, object-less euphoria while eliminating disorientation, dehydration, increased fat storage, cell mutations, headaches, hangovers, and withdrawal. Ethanol is a hell of a toxin.

While I sit here writing this, I feel more alive and more euphoric than I ever did during my drinking years. Of course it's possible to feel good without booze - don't you remember running around for no reason when you were a kid? Alcohol monopolizes positive emotions that you used to take for granted as natural daily occurrences. Now it's time to break up alcohol's sinister monopoly over your brain.

Dominating Alcohol Addiction is Heroic

I did not discover until I quit drinking that I was almost certainly genetically predisposed to alcohol addiction. I was adopted at birth and knew nothing about my birth parents. After consulting with doctors, I discovered that I had been exposed to large amounts of alcohol in the womb. Alcohol exposure caused a hearing impairment that I had long regarded as a random fact of life.

Like many other people who have recovered, I see in retrospect that I had a problem with alcohol from the very first time that I drank. I had always assumed that I was firmly in control of my behavior. I didn't particularly resent anyone and I didn't habitually lie, cheat, steal, or do anything else that would evoke the "addict" label. It took a decade for alcohol to affect my relationships and my career.

Not many people enjoy a happy childhood, excel in school, develop great friendships, and then start climbing the ladder to success, only to realize that their biggest obstacle in life was waiting to bite them in the ass all along.

I suspect that I'm far from unique in this way. Perhaps you swore early in life never to drink like your mom or your dad, and yet here you are anyway. Do not feel shame, which is a worthless emotion that poisons the mind. Since alcohol addiction is a biochemical disorder, there is nothing you could have done to prevent it except to refuse the first drink you ever took. You were raised in a culture dominated by alcoholic ads, parties, and people; one in which adults ask each other, "Why aren't you drinking?" far more often than "Why are you drinking?" How likely would you have been to decide to teetotal for no reason?

Now, of course, you have a reason. And it's not because you're an "alcoholic" who has to miss out on all the fun from now on. It's quite the opposite, actually.

It's because you're slowly realizing that drinking sucks. You're opening your eyes, standing up and getting off of the drunken merry go-around that's built on quicksand. You have no interest in finding out whether you could be one of the lucky ones who escapes death and merely goes through life more irritable, more sleep-deprived, more susceptible to cancer, and more miserable on Saturday mornings than you would be if you didn't drink at all.

Dominating alcohol won't confine you to a life of misunderstood stoicism. There's real pleasure and real happiness on the other side. But first, you'll have to stabilize your system...

CHAPTER 3

REPAIR YOUR BRAIN

"A stable mind is impossible without a balanced brain."
-Dr. Linus Pauling, Two-Time Nobel Prize Winner

We are told that relapse is a normal part of recovering from addiction. Nothing could be further from the truth.

Would you believe me if I told you that three out of every four relapses could be prevented with supplements you can get over the counter? Several years ago, I wouldn't have believed this either. Let me explain.

People don't relapse because they've failed to be honest with themselves. In most cases, they turn back to alcohol because they're anxious and depressed. They feel this way because alcohol fundamentally altered their physiology, making it impossible for them to feel good about anything. As we will see, this damage can be reversed if it is addressed with certain supplements.

Abstinence often brings people back to square one. They know subconsciously that for all of its toxic effects, alcohol temporarily balances their brain chemistry. They derive tremendous amounts of energy from alcohol, rather than the disorientation and sedation that light drinkers experience. Alcohol seems to be the only thing that can erase the harsh lows that it creates. Many people who call themselves "recovering alcoholics" instinctively know that no amount of group therapy will make them feel better than drinking does.

No one tells them about the nutritional supplements that can repair alcohol's damage. No one tells them that common nutrients can provide them with energy they used to get from alcohol and alleviate their anxiety and depression. Nutrition is a major piece of solving the addiction puzzle. To recover, life needs to feel livable again.

After about a dozen failed attempts to quit drinking, I once concluded that I was special. I'm so smart that I need alcohol to dumb reality down for me. Grocery shopping, talking to strangers in the elevator, doing boring work - all of these were so boring for me that I needed alcohol to get through them. I could go a week without drinking at this point, and so I clearly wasn't an "alcoholic" - I was just special.

The truth was that while I hadn't experienced enough kindling to have a seizure from withdrawal, I was so addicted to alcohol that I could not enjoy simple things without it. I had depleted my brain chemicals, and my reality without alcohol seemed like an old, sad, black and white movie playing in fast motion.

I have no doubt, looking back, that nutrient reloading and amino acid supplementation at this point in my life would have made the small things in life enjoyable once again. This is exactly what supplementation did for me once I finally quit drinking and decided to tackle my health from the inside out. As I balanced my brain on a molecular level, life became a full color movie once again.

If you only drank a bottle of wine per night, you will need less repair than someone who drank a handle of hard alcohol each day. Either way, drinking heavily for prolonged periods creates invisible wounds that time will not heal. Because alcohol leaches so many nutrients from the body, it's simply not enough to eat healthy.

Many people who haven't had a drink in years have never repaired their systems. I recall listening to a man in AA, who said he had been sober for five years, talking about how he still fought intense cravings every day. He prayed and told himself that one day he might be able to drink again, concluding that he would stay sober for today.

I know now that this tortured soul almost certainly suffered from nutrient deficiencies. If he's still alive, he's one of hundreds of thousands out there with the same basic problem. People who are treated for alcohol addiction have mortality rates that are about the same as those who keep drinking: about three times that of the normal population. One in four commit suicide and many others succumb to cancer and heart disease from years of drinking.

Our medical establishment is slowly realizing that brain health depends in large part on our bodily health. There are more serotonin receptors in our digestive tract than in our brains, and gut conditions like candida (which affect a large percentage of alcoholics) can literally hijack our emotions. Heavy drinking severely damages the intestinal tract, resulting in poor nutrient absorption. Many addiction treatment centers slap a "cross-addiction" warning on lifting weights, while saying nothing about 2-liter per day soda habits that trap many people in hypoglycemic hell.

We didn't evolve to be anxious, depressed, or fatigued. These are not our natural states, nor are we born into Prozac deficiency.

Nutritional supplements are extremely safe. Give them a try before turning to harsh prescription medicines, which slap bandaids on your symptoms rather than enabling your body to fix the root causes of your problems.

Nutritional Epiphanies

When I quit drinking, I decided to tackle my health holistically. I thought of it as a separate project that had little to do with beating addiction. I had always taken pride in my fitness and I wanted to look and feel the way I did before I ruined my body with alcohol. After detoxing with benzodiazepines, I started taking B-vitamins, a men's sports multivitamin, and omega-3 fish oil.

I soon realized that I had some of the hallmark symptoms of magnesium deficiency: restlessness, low-level anxiety, and trouble sleeping. On a whim, I ordered magnesium taurate from Amazon. I took it one evening, expecting nothing. I drifted into the calmest sleep I'd had in years and I felt more relaxed from that point onward. This one supplement created a "new normal" for my level of daily functioning that I now take for granted.

A few months later, Mother Nature sabotaged my plan to start an outdoor bootcamp. As it rained for nearly two weeks straight, I felt mildly depressed and started having irrational thoughts about drinking. I started to wonder whether I was upset about the bootcamp or simply deprived of sun. I resolved my dilemma by taking Vitamin D3, which cured my bad mood in a single afternoon. This is one of the few supplements I still take on an ongoing basis, but only when I've missed a few days of sun.

It occurred to me that if supplementation can help treat anxiety and depression, it should be able to help prevent relapses caused by these very things. I had no research to back up my conviction except for a study on the positive effects of Vitamin B3 for people recovering from alcohol addiction.

About 2 years after my last drink, I read a book called *7 Weeks to Sobriety* out of pure curiosity. Its author is Joan Mathews Larson, an addiction expert who lost her son to suicide after he completed as 12-Step based treatment program. In 1981, she founded a treatment center called Health Recovery Center (HRC) that still operates today and which has successfully treated thousands of alcoholics through biochemical repair.

Finally, I had some evidence to back up my hunch about the role of nutrition in conquering addiction. By discharge, most HRC patients have not only detoxed but totally avoided the symptoms of post-acute withdrawal syndrome that lead to relapse:

- **89%** have no anxiety
- **94%** have no insomnia
- **98%** have no shakiness
- **95%** are depression-free

After three and a half years, about 75% of HRC's clients are still abstinent. Compare this number to 10-25% for conventional treatment centers.

By the time I discovered Dr. Larson's book, I had already taken many of the supplements she recommends. My epiphany consisted of the realization that there was a workable theory and real-life results that could guide the kind of intelligent experimentation I had done.

Is it a coincidence that I achieved a new normal of daily functioning with each supplement that worked for me? Is it a coincidence that my drinking dreams and occasional alcohol thoughts disappeared soon after I began supplementing with amino acids? It's possible that all I needed was time to rewire my brain. But the weight of the evidence supporting biochemical repair - and the long line of obviously real 5 Star Amazon reviews for Dr. Larson's book - would suggest otherwise.

HRC uses megadoses of specific nutrients to treat patients who are detoxifying. Perhaps my results would have been better with megadoses. I achieved them nonetheless with the maximum recommended dosages of supplements I had bought well before I found Dr. Larson's book.

The Essentials of Brain Repair

Below I will share the 10 supplements that helped me to conquer alcohol cravings forever and repair my body. If I knew what I know now when I quit drinking, I would have started taking all of them as soon as I finished my last sip of alcohol. But it is never too late to repair your system, even if you quit drinking long ago.

My recommendation is to take all of these supplements together for 30 days. You don't have to take any of them forever. Once you've replenished your system, you can take them only on an as-needed basis.

Consult your doctor before deciding to take vitamins or nutritional supplements.

Multivitamin / Multimineral: Most multivitamins are scams that cram as many synthetic nutrients as possible into a stinky pill that never gets absorbed into your body. After wasting a lot of money, I shunned them all. And then I tried Legion Triumph, which increased my energy levels and helped me sleep. Triumph is designed to replace nutrients that athletes lose through sweating. Because alcohol is a poison and a diuretic, heavy drinkers lose more nutrients than athletes. A few extra supplements are still required.

B-Vitamin Complex: People who drink heavily quickly deplete B-Vitamins that are necessary for energy levels and to ward off depression. Extra high levels of niacin, pantothenic acid, thiamine and folic acid have been proven to aid in biochemical repair. I took the recommended dosage of a standard B-Complex for 6 months after I quit drinking.

Vitamin C: Huge amounts of this vitamin have been shown to be nontoxic and to ease withdrawal significantly. It has an almost magical ability to repair every cell in your body. I did not take enough vitamin C until nearly a year after I quit drinking. I recommend taking the maximum dosage of liposomal vitamin C, which absorbs better than other vitamin C supplements.

Vitamin D3: The sun vitamin is involved in so many bodily processes that it's more of a hormone than a vitamin. Heavy drinkers almost always have a severe deficiency of Vitamin D, causing fatigue and stress. To this day, I take the recommended dosage of vitamin D3 when I haven't had enough natural sun.

Magnesium: Magnesium was my "miracle" supplement - I noticed a difference right away in my ability to relax and fall asleep. Unfortunately, the most common brands in the stores is magnesium oxide, which does not absorb well and has laxative effects. I recommend magnesium citrate because it is very well-absorbed.

Omega-3 Fish Oil: The majority of your brain tissue is composed of fat, and taking omega-3 fatty acids can help regenerate it. Heavy drinkers and many depressed people tend to be severely deficient in essential fatty acids (EFAs). Supplementation can reduce depression and anxiety and improve cognitive function. It's difficult to get enough omega-3's from eating fish.

(I'll note here that some people have been cured of alcohol addiction by taking GLA, another fatty acid that restores a brain chemical that they are genetically unable to produce. This deficiency cruelly leads them back to the bottle for relief until they identify this root cause of their behavior. If you have always felt depressed, even before you started drinking, look into GLA supplementation.)

L-Glutamine: This amino acid has been proven to reduce alcohol cravings on day one. Even if you've quit drinking long ago, you can benefit from reduced levels of anxiety, better sleep quality, and improved muscle synthesis. Athletes take L-Glutamine to help them recover from tough workouts. This nutrient will help your fitness as much as it helps to restore your brain health.

L-Tyrosine: This amino acid is used in the brain to produce neurotransmitters called catecholamines, among them dopamine and norepinephrine. It can reverse dopamine deficiency and improve stress response. It has a mild stimulatory effect and should be taken in the morning or early afternoon. When I take l-tyrosine, my desire to drink coffee is reduced. Amino acids like l-tyrosine are not drugs; they are building blocks that your body uses to produces hormones and neurotransmitters. Supplementing with l-tyrosine for 30 days can help you to improve your motivation by restoring natural chemicals that keep anxiety, stress, and depression at bay. This amino acid requires nutrients found in a multivitamin in order to be synthesized properly by your body.

DL-Phenylalanine: A blend of two amino acids, dl-phenylalanine is often used to treat alcohol and opiate withdrawal. It improves nerve cell communication, reduces pain, and aids in the production of neurotransmitters that reduce depression. While l-tyrosine improves my motivation, dl-phenylalanine makes me feel calm and content. I do not take them both at the same time. I recommend taking l-tyrosine upon waking and dl-phenylalanine after lunch to help avoid a midday slump. This amino acid will not merely enhance your daily functioning; it will help your brain produce natural chemicals that you drowned with alcohol.

L-Tryptophan: This amino acid is the building block of serotonin, which is necessary for feeling calm and sleeping well. I have had better results taking 5HTP than L-tryptophan, but preferences vary from person to person. L-tryptophan is converted into 5HTP by your body, so take one or the other and not both! These supplements should be taken before bed because they can make you drowsy. Over time they will help you to replenish your natural supply of serotonin. By empowering your system in this way, you'll be less likely to turn to drugs that provide temporary relief while depleting your serotonin levels in the long run.

(Want to see my current brand preferences for the basic supplements outlined above? Simply go to **Fit-Recovery.com/DrinkingSucks** and use **DrinkingSucks** as the password.)

Some important nutrients, like zinc, are omitted from this list because most powerful multivitamins already contain them in sufficient amounts. Others, like calcium, are omitted because most people get enough from their diets.

Don't ignore the amino acids simply because they have confusing names. They can help to restore neurotransmitter balance in a miraculous way. Be sure to stay within the recommended dosage though; I once took three times the recommended dosage of l-tryptophan one evening and felt strange.

Do not take l-tryptophan or 5HTP if you take antidepressants. Doing so can lead to a dangerous condition called serotonin syndrome. If you take medications or have any other health problems, discuss them first with your doctor.

Biochemical balance is a precondition for exercising free will. I'll let you in on a little secret: I continued taking DL-Phenylalanine for three months after repairing my brain with the other supplements. I still use it when I feel like I'm lagging. It helped me to achieve a positive outlook on more days than I can count, and I might not have had the energy or optimism to write this book if I had not discovered it.

It might have occurred to your clever brain that if the nutrients above can help you repair from alcohol-induced damage, perhaps they can be used as maintenance to keep you healthy while you keep drinking! Unless you're trying The Sinclair Method under a doctor's guidance, this is a terrible idea. Drinking inhibits the absorption of nutrients, so the vast majority of the supplements will be immediately flushed out of your system along with the alcohol you continue to consume. Moreover, the progressive nature of alcohol addiction guarantees that the amount you drink will eventually negate any benefit you get from supplementation.

You might be concerned about the expense of buying 10 supplements at once. But ask yourself: what price do you put on repairing your body and permanently extinguishing the desire to drink? Is it less than what you were you spending on alcohol every month before you quit drinking? If investing a few hundred dollars in your health today can help you avert relapse later and save you from unexpectedly spending $20,000 (or much more) for rehab, is it worth a try? Of course it is.

The supplements I've recommended have been used by thousands of people to recover. You might be thinking, what's so groundbreaking about common nutrients like Vitamin C or magnesium? The answer is simple. The benefits of basic, high quality nutrients go unnoticed in the sea of Internet hype over snake oil wrapped in shiny new packaging.

Don't run out and start megadosing every nutrient you can find. More is not always better. There are certain nutrients, like Vitamin A and Vitamin E, that should never be consumed in high doses. Be sure to buy high quality supplements. Low quality ones are often diluted with sketchy fillers and ingredients that aren't even listed on the labels.

I use Amazon Prime to purchase my supplements, and I take advantage of subscription prices for the few that I use on an ongoing basis.

Don't be among the majority of "recovering alcoholics" with a sad demeanor and a bland sense of life. The supplements above can help you finally feel good without alcohol for less than you typically spent on alcohol in a month. Maybe I'm wrong, and maybe they won't work for you. Maybe your body responds better to prayer. All I can say is that every supplement I've listed absolutely worked for me.

You're the only person who can give your body what it needs to adapt to life without alcohol in the shortest time possible. Alcohol addiction is not a choice, but the will to recover certainly is. What would happen if you empowered every cell in your body to keep you recovered forever?

CHAPTER 4

STABILIZE YOUR DIET

"The higher your energy level, the more efficient your body. The more efficient your body, the better you feel and the more you will use your talent to produce outstanding results. "
-Tony Robbins

A few years ago, I agreed to get coffee with a friend who hadn't had a drink in 6 months. He told me self-evidently that he had an "addict brain" and that he often asked God for peace of mind. I remember watching him pour about half a cup of sugar into his coffee. He did the same thing for his second cup about 10 minutes later. I thought to myself, that's more table sugar than I consume in a year.

Why wait for supernatural forces to give you things that you have the power to achieve on your own? There's a good chance that my friend could achieve peace of mind naturally. Reducing his sugar intake would be a good place to start. He had apparently never learned about the devastating mental health consequences of excessive sugar intake. Stevia is a great substitute for sugar and unlike artificial sweeteners, it actually has documented health benefits.

We already know that what we put into our bodies can break us. When we put alcohol into our bodies, we became an unstable mixture of anxiety and incoherence. Greasy processed carbs and soda will have a similar effect, making it impossible for you to experience the benefits of removing alcohol from your life.

A better diet correlates with mental stability, a reduced chance of relapse, and a more positive experience of life. It's been said that diet determines 75% of your physique. I would bet that it determines an even higher percentage of your sense of well-being. In this chapter, I'm going to show you some simple methods for developing eating habits that can help you feel upbeat every day.

The Problem With Diets

Most people want to eat better. They make resolutions and try unsustainable starvation diets. After these moments pass, their subconscious minds take over. Most of them continue to reach for sugar highs and artificial flavors instead of the real foods our bodies evolved to consume.

If you subject your body and brain to a pendulum of sugar highs and crashes, your moods will mimic the ups and downs of alcohol addiction. Since alcohol is the most easily absorbed form of sugar, your alcohol cravings will persist far into the future. If you fill your body with trans fats and preservatives from fast food, you'll feel sluggish and depressed.

Your willpower reserve is limited, which is to say that you can only put up with so much frustration in one day. If you try to starve yourself periodically to make up for bad food choices that are your default eating habits, you'll diminish willpower that could have been used to accomplish other goals.

Failing a diet can be disastrous for your internal sense of self-efficacy. This is the reason that so many people who quit drinking refuse to address nutrition. They're afraid that failing will send them back into the spiral of addiction. Some of them decry societal pressure to lose weight. But the relationship between what you put into your body and how you feel is not a mystery. Fat loss should not be your only goal in eating better, and there's nothing wrong with striving to become lean. Happy, physically glowing people have figured out for themselves that they feel better when they eat natural foods with more nutrient density.

The truth is that you don't need to follow a strict diet to get healthy and start feeling better about yourself. Develop new habits that can be sustained for the long term.

It took several years of trial and error before I developed a set of sustainable eating habits. I'm sure that some of them are subjective to the point of being bizarre. They work for me; the key is to find out what works for you.

We all have different bodies, different genes, and we respond to foods differently. Some people do well without grains. (I'm not one of them, perhaps because my Scottish ancestors thrived on porridge.) Some people are mildly allergic to dairy and their lives improve drastically when they cut out milk and cheese.

Find out what foods fit your preferences and your body chemistry and make them long-term staples.

Master the Art of Food Substitution

If you fill your refrigerator with health foods that make you gag, you'll end up ordering pizza every night and letting the weird stuff rot on the shelves.

Most people eat fewer than 20 foods on a regular basis. Small substitutions can lead to drastic improvements over the course of weeks, months, and years. You don't have to start ordering boring salads at restaurants as long as you boost the QUALITY of the foods sitting in your kitchen.

If you don't prepare the majority of your own food, you should start today. There's no way to know what restaurants (and especially delis) are putting into your food. The only reliable way to keep junk out of your stomach is the keep it out of your kitchen and learn how to cook simple meals.

Once you stabilize your brain with the nutrients in the previous chapter, you'll notice that you have a bit more willpower. Use this extra willpower to kick out some of your more egregious food choices and replace them with healthy alternatives that still taste good to you.

I'll give you some examples from my experience. All of the food choices below are current staples for me. Your list might not look anything like mine. There's a healthy substitute for every unhealthy food, but there's no substitute for figuring out what works for your body and what you'll actually eat.

- **Sprouted grains**: I used to make sandwiches on "100% whole wheat bread" and always felt bloated afterwards. Since switching to Ezekiel bread, my energy and digestion are much better.

- **Grass fed butter**: Ordinary white butter comes from cows that don't eat grass and miss out on important nutrients. Pasture butter contains CLA and Vitamin K2, nutrients that unclog your arteries.

- **Organic dark chocolate**: Look for brands made with real butter instead of emulsifying chemicals. Instead of impulsively buying snickers bars, I began substituting 85% dark chocolate sweetened with stevia and monkfruit.

- **Grass fed beef and bison**: Good red meat contains healthy fats and can be better for you than chicken.

- **Exotic spices and hot peppers**: Capsaicin, which makes peppers hot, releases endorphins and kills viruses, bacteria, and cancer cells.

- **Organic nut butter**: Use these on toast or celery instead of products that have added sugar and hydrogenated oils in them.

- **Kombucha, La Croix, and Zevia**: These are great substitutes for common sodas. Regular soda and diet soda pollute your body with chemicals.

- **Fresh produce on sale:** If you have an adventurous spirit like I do, channel it into the produce aisle. My snacks are vegetables with hummus made without soybean oil or dip made with Greek yogurt and spices.

- **Juicing**: A juicer will give you an extra incentive to buy fresh produce. None of your fruits and vegetables will go bad when you can turn them into fresh juice before they expire.

- **Organic Sauerkraut**: You can find this in the refrigerated section of health stores like Whole Foods. Unlike the canned version, it's a great source of probiotics.

Honestly, my food substitutions taste way better to me now than the crap that I used to eat. I take pride in the fact that every cell in my body is now made from higher quality raw materials.

Out with the old, in with the new:

- ~~Diet Soda~~ **Zevia / Low Sugar Kombucha / La Croix / Waterloo / Unsweetened Tea**

- ~~Junk Snacks~~ **Epic Beef Bites**

- ~~Coffee With Cream And Sugar~~ **Coffee With Unsweetened Coconut Milk And Stevia**

- ~~French Fries~~ **Baked Yam Wedges / Air-Popped Sweet Potatoes**

- ~~Corn Flakes~~ **Steel-Cut Oat Parfait With Berries / Chia Seed Pudding**

- ~~Ice Cream~~ **Fresh Berries With Whipped Heavy Cream And Stevia**

- ~~McDonald's Hamburger~~ **Bison Burger On Ezekial Sprouted English Muffin**

- ~~Frozen Hot Pocket~~ **Scrambled Eggs And A Banana**

- ~~Fish Sticks And Fries~~ **Baked Salmon And Lentils**

- ~~Orange Juice~~ **Morning Smoothie***

- ~~Cereal With Skim Milk~~ **Grass-Fed Ribeye And Eggs**

- ~~Bagel With Cream Cheese~~ **Ezekiel Sprouted Bread With Coconut Oil, Stevia, And Cinnamon**

- ~~Frozen Creamed Spinach~~ **Flash-Frozen Greens Sautéed In Extra-Virgin Olive Oil (With Garlic)**

*C's Morning Smoothie Recipe: 1 Cup Unsweetened Coconut Milk, Banana, 1/2 Cup Frozen Wild Blueberries, 1 Scoop Organic Beet Powder, 1 Scoop Organic Greens Powder, 1 Tablespoon Maca Powder.

(If I'm feeling ambitious, I'll add some frozen broccoli sprouts or fresh ginger and turmeric into my smoothie as well. I don't have any particular brand loyalty for beet powder and organic greens powder, as there are a variety of brands with great reviews on Amazon.)

Here's a good rule of thumb: Any food in your Top 20 that contains artificial flavors should be replaced. You don't have to banish anything forever, but there's always a natural substitute that tastes better and satisfies you for longer. Artificial flavors - found in fast food, prepackaged snacks, and frozen meals - trick your brain into thinking that nutrition is on its way. When it doesn't come, you simply crave more. Have you ever seen anyone eat 3 cantaloupes? Probably not, but you see people put away 3 large bags of chips all the time.

I'll be the first to admit that I don't always follow my own advice. Recently, I had a few weeks in a row in which I started eating ice cream before bed. I began waking up with pounding headaches. Instead of banishing ice cream forever, I started eating toasted Ezekiel with grass fed butter and organic honey instead. Within a few days, I stopped craving any food before bed.

With Substitutes In Place, You Can Eat Instinctively

I used to set up artificial eating schedules and try to stick to them. Now I prefer to listen to what my body is telling me. This may seem strange, but on some days I'll have six meals and on others, I'll only have two.

Diet gurus tend to ignore the reality of our experience when we get hungry. What do we do when we feel that pang in our stomach and start salivating? We think about what we have in the house or in the office to eat. If we think "eh," we consider going across the street for a huge burrito, stopping at the grocery store or ordering pizza from a delivery place.

When we're hungry, we don't really want to stop at a green juice bar or drive to the store to buy just one piece of fish to bring home and cook. The key is to negate the "eh" feeling by having plenty of food available when we're ready to eat, wherever we happen to be. Most offices have kitchens. Even if yours doesn't, it's easy to pack a small cooler with your healthy substitutes and an ice pack.

If you don't have the patience to cook intricate recipes, we have something in common. The easiest methods of preparation are often the best. The other day, I got a pound of grass fed beef on sale and cooked it in a cast iron pan with a diced sweet potato, a diced yellow onion, Himalayan salt and Cajun spices. That whole meal cost me $8, took 10 minutes to make and lasted for two sittings. Fish filets can be taken out of the freezer, defrosted in a bowl of water in 10 minutes, spiced up and then sautéed with olive oil. They always go well over spinach tossed with balsamic vinegar, and perhaps some basmati rice on the side.

I could go on for ten pages with delicious and healthy recipes that nonetheless don't belong in gourmet cookbooks, but you might get annoyed with me. My point is that sometimes you have to visualize the simplest of processes before you realize they're possible.

The benefits of intermittent fasting and time-restricted eating are well documented, and I have a lot of unplanned fasts. I tend to skip breakfast after I've gone out for a big dinner, because I'm simply not hungry until 1 PM the next day. Or I might have a big breakfast and not eat until 8 PM that night. You don't have to count calories or sacrifice big meals if you listen to your body.

...And Live A Little

Now I'm going to tell you something that makes me sound like a hypocrite: I eat things like fried chicken, biscuits, ice cream and pie every week. I have an all-out cheat meal every Sunday evening that is my first and only meal of that day. I feel bloated afterwards, but it's worth it. I'm not training for a bodybuilding competition. I'm trying to live life to the fullest.

You can eat your favorite fatty and sugary meals without destroying your health if you only have them once per week. The secrets that make this possible are fasting beforehand, and planning cheat meals in advance. It doesn't feel like you're sacrificing anything when you always have a cheat meal to look forward to.

I tend to spend most of my appetite on various meats, rather than ice cream, so I rarely wake up with a headache on Mondays.

Get High in the Morning

Life is meant to be enjoyed, not endured. The philosophy of substitution that applies to food choices also applies to the natural highs we choose. There's nothing wrong with looking forward to waking up and making coffee or tea every morning in the same way that you used to enjoy getting home from work and opening up a bottle of wine. The habit may feel similar but they're not the same thing at all. Coffee increases your productivity and infuses your body with antioxidants. Alcohol is a toxin with exaggerated health benefits, which are negated by its risks for anyone predisposed to addiction.

Just like exercising, coffee is much more satisfying for me as a nondrinker. Having a better sense of taste is probably part of the reason, since drinking can dull your sense of taste for days. I now see that morning coffee high as a treasure. That rush of energy shouldn't be wasted on pointless TV shows or aimless web surfing sessions.

I'm aware that some addiction professionals frown at caffeine. I agree that too much caffeine can be problematic for stress chemical regulation. But I've never had a problem with it. Coffee contains anti-cancer properties, protects your liver, boosts your mood and mental performance, and reduces diabetes risk. Since it takes 8 hours for caffeine to leave your system, it's best to stop drinking coffee at noon so that you don't have trouble sleeping.

If you're sensitive to caffeine, then coffee may not be the way to go. I once read about a woman who thought she was going insane - until she cut out coffee. Everyone is different. If you're averse to caffeine, then you should know that herbal teas contain a host of health benefits, mood-boosting properties, and anti-aging compounds. The principle remains the same: Experiment with new beverages and figure out what works best for you! Reclaim your mornings and start enjoying them ASAP!

CHAPTER 5

REBUILD YOUR BODY

"What we face may look insurmountable. But I learned something from all those sets and reps when I didn't think I could lift another weight. What I learned is that we are always stronger than we know. "
-Arnold Schwarzenegger

You now understand the biochemical roots of alcohol addiction. You know which nutrients are necessary to repair your body from years of drinking and what kind of foods will support your transformation. Now it's time to train your brain to produce natural reward chemicals, including endorphins, without drinking.

When you quit drinking, your entire body may seem to scream for alcohol. Nutrient repair breaks physical cravings, but exercise speeds up the process by providing a powerful natural high. Before we install Drinking Sucks 2.0 onto the operating system of your mind, we will reboot your entire brain-body system, obliterating the faulty piece of coding that tricks your brain into thinking, in any given moment, that drinking is the surest path to pleasure.

Exercise is a powerful weapon against destructive brain impulses. It does not need to become the center of your life, just a part of your lifestyle. Working out is an incredibly effective catalyst for dismantling alcohol's grip on your psyche. Its benefits will accumulate and stay with you long after alcohol loses its power over your subconscious thoughts.

Over time, exercise overwrites your brain's association between alcohol and reward chemicals. It helps you to create new associations between healthy activities and those same reward chemicals. It floods your body with endorphins and anti-stress chemicals that allow you relax during the day and sleep at night. It reverses long-lasting brain damage caused by alcohol and increases the flow of oxygen to your brain, helping you to think more clearly.

Exercise-induced transient hypofrontality is a state in which working out deactivates the prefrontal cortex. A rush of neurotransmitters heightens your sense of well-being and shifts you into a more relaxed and creative plane of consciousness. Although the prefrontal cortex is necessary for rational decision making, hyperactivity in this region is the source of racing thoughts, self-criticism, and negative thinking. Hypofrontality is currently the subject of extensive research, but many people who lift weights or who enjoy "runners' high" can confirm this effect from experience.

One of my personal training clients, a high stress individual who used to drink too much, told me the other day: "My prefrontal cortex is freaking out…Time to put my dukes up!" A few months earlier, she might have reached for a bottle of wine and cancelled her session. She finished the workout looking relaxed and visibly glowing.

What benefits our physiology also heals our minds. Our bodies are the only vehicles we will ever have to experience life. Rebuilding your body when you beat addiction is a no-brainer, pun intended.

In 2011, Frontiers in Psychiatry conducted a study on the efficacy of using exercise to fight substance addiction. The researchers concluded, "Enough is now known to begin the process of designing and implementing exercise-based interventions."

A Missing Piece of The Puzzle

So where are these exercise-based interventions? You won't find them, because the Minnesota Model of treatment addiction (the one used in 90% of centers) has very little to say about exercise. You'd think from reading treatment center blogs that your goal in life is to sit still forever; that the unique duty of permanently recovering addicts is to exist WITHOUT pleasure, thrills, or intensity. You'd think that the goal for people who can't moderate anything is to learn how to either abstain from or moderate everything before they die. If I'd let myself buy into this, I would have relapsed before I'd finished detoxing.

When you're in the best shape of your life - and improving, week after week - you have a very powerful reason to avoid drinking. You'll begin to see your body as the vehicle for everything you want to accomplish in life. As your self-image improves, you'll become careful not to contaminate your hard-won progress. You'll take more pride in everything you do.

Some people will scoff and say this mindset is narcissistic. Often these people like to brood about their past without offering any solutions they've found that could help other people. One of my former Twitter followers exploded and unfollowed me after I wrote that lifting weights helped me quit drinking for good. He went on a bizarre rant about surrendering to God and protein powder addiction. For whatever reason, he harbored some serious resentment toward those of us who choose self-improvement over recovery slogans.

Alcoholic Workouts Are Not The Same

Going to the gym was a drag before I quit drinking. If I pushed through the pain for long enough, I'd get a mild endorphin rush that might keep me from drinking for an extra couple of hours. When I finally worked up a sweat, I could feel ethanol seeping out of my pores. My abdomen ached below the right side of my rib cage, which I later identified as a symptom of pancreas inflammation. I was painfully dehydrated, despite drinking water all day. I would look at my puffy cheeks and glazed red eyes in the mirror, hoping that my

CHRIS SCOTT

old gritty self was somewhere to be found behind the hideous mask that alcohol had plastered onto my face.

My workouts were depressing: I rarely summoned the energy to do more than 50% of my supposed max on any lift. I never fully recovered from my last workout. Occasionally I would do some abs, hoping they might suddenly appear despite being drowned in poison every night.

Sometimes I'd go for a jog and ruminate on all of the reasons I should stop drinking immediately. After passing cafes and seeing people pour wine, I would convince myself that I couldn't have a problem because I was working out while they were drinking! I'd stop at a liquor store in my jogging outfit and return home with a huge bottle of vodka, which has fewer calories than wine - a decision I could be proud of, because I wanted to be healthy.

Working out alone is not sufficient to make you quit drinking. Exercise is a piece of the puzzle that only fits once you stop drinking. The quality of your workouts, and of your ensuing mood boost, will skyrocket the longer you stay away from alcohol. Working out these days feels nothing like it did when I was still drinking.

...Lifting Weights Is SO MUCH BETTER As A Nondrinker

Several years after my toxin-infused lifting sessions, I inhabit a much different universe. I regularly lift weights, run sprints, go for bike rides, and spar with a partner in boxing and Muay Thai. I like learning new forms of exercise because I want to push my boundaries. As with restrictive diets, beware any guru who tells you there's only one way to get fit.

Weightlifting is my favorite form of exercise. If building strength is your goal, you will want to lift weights in some form. My workouts center around compound powerlifting exercises like deadlifts, bench presses, squats, and rows. I'll focus on one compound lift per workout and then hit the same muscle group with different exercises. My routines are constantly changing and I draw from kettlebell

56

programs, Olympic lifts, TRX, and CrossFit workouts.

I can tell you that nothing on earth is like the experience of lifting heavy weights. The word "heavy" is obviously a relative term - it describes a weight that you can handle for only 1-6 repetitions.

These days I look forward to driving to the gym as much as I look forward to making coffee in the morning. I'm excited to see how hard I can push myself today. I'm looking forward to banishing the mundane thoughts that occasionally cloud my mind. I can't wait to feel the hard-earned euphoria.

On my first few sets I'm still breaking the ice. Soon I'm going into steady focus mode. I'm taking more oxygen into my body and totally inhabiting the present moment. As I add more weight and start numbing to the pain, I'm entering warrior mode. No one in this gym can touch me. I'll hit the heaviest of my sets and feel my nervous system release every ounce of stress I'd been holding onto. Eyes begin to refocus in my direction. My last set ends with a euphoric buzz that sees me through the rest of my workout. The high lasts for several hours afterwards, sustaining me until I'm ready to collapse into my bed like a grizzly bear ready for hibernation.

This is how it feels to lift weights several years after you've quit drinking. It may take you a few months before you even begin to feel what I'm talking about. If you've ever wondered why some people have the willpower to hit the gym day after day, week after week, you should know that it has nothing to do with willpower. They aren't genetic warriors with a higher pain threshold. They have rewired their brains to anticipate the endorphin rush and they have reframed the gym as their shrine. They see weightlifting as their meditation and therapy wrapped into one activity with a myriad of other health and aesthetic benefits.

Once you rewire your brain in this way, it will take willpower to decide not to do your workouts.

Still not convinced that your brain is that malleable? I used to hate doing deadlifts, or anything legs-related for that matter. These days, you could say that heavy deadlifts are my Xanax.

Strength and Physique Improvement

If you're just starting out in the gym, aim for three sets of 10 reps for compound exercises. Deadlifts, squats, rows, dips, pull-ups, bench press - any exercise that works more than one muscle group. Rest for a minute between exercises and try to make your workouts last for 45 minutes. Your goal should be to learn proper form and develop muscle memory for your exercises. I've had great results using this program three times per week for 4 weeks with new personal training clients.

Strength training is the next step. Increase the weight and aim for 5 sets of 5. Add some isolated exercises - like curls, tricep extension, leg curls - especially for muscles that are your weakest points. Rest for one to two minutes between sets and lift for an hour. This kind of training can be done up to 5 times per week as long as you never train the same muscle group two days in a row. Over time and with a spotter, you can test lower rep ranges and discover your one-rep maxes.

I alternate 6 weeks of strength training with 6 weeks of German Volume Training (GVT), after which I'll take a week off to let my nervous system recover. GVT was invented by a hardcore weightlifter in East Germany in the 1970s. It involves 10 sets of 10 reps for one exercise per workout. Your muscles will get bigger and you will experience a pump that lasts for hours after each workout. This program should not be attempted by beginners, and its proper methodology is the subject of many ridiculous online rants. I do the 10 x 10 for one compound lift at the beginning of each workout, resting for one minute between sets. I'll then spend the rest of my workout doing 3 x 10 for isolated exercises.

Whether I'm doing low rep strength training or higher rep GVT, I'll get creative toward the end of each workout. I'll sample new ab exercises or do padded ball slam downs, weighted box jumps, or other exercises that target the muscle group I'm working that day. I keep my workouts centered and focused around my main lifts, yet fresh and flexible.

Cardio and Diversifying Your Workouts

Most people hate doing cardio. I've learned that if you start slow and short and add pace and distance, over time you will come to enjoy the workouts. Runners' high is an altogether different and equally satisfying experience as heavy lifting euphoria. Our bodies evolved to experience both of them.

Research shows that high intensity interval training (HIIT) burns more fat and preserves more muscle than steady-state cardio. My intuition tells me that there's a place for every form of exercise, and my life experience is more important to me than studies on fat cells. On some days I'll do sprints outside and on others, I'll have a 45 minute energy-sapping sparring session. I prefer to do cardio first thing in the morning to help me wake up and tackle the day.

On weekends, I'll sometimes open the door and just walk for an hour. Walking is underrated. It's a great opportunity to listen to nature or get into an audiobook.

Workouts mix well with adventure and wanderlust. I had a blast with some friends at a rock climbing gym last year. I've since moved to the coast and plan to try paddle boarding. On weekends, I'll go for a long bike ride without headphones to feel connected with nature. If you're interested in martial arts like I am, you can take Krav Maga classes, join a BJJ gym, or learn how to box.

If you're at a loss for adding variety to your workouts, it's not a bad idea to peruse YouTube. I'll admit that I've added some celebrity workouts to my routine to keep things interesting. I grew up practicing Tae Kwon Do and Scott Adkins' videos helped motivate me to regain some of my old skills. There are some entertaining videos on how to do handstand pushups and backflips. Why not set out to accomplish some new physical goals?

Above all, you need to get the hell out of your house every day. If you're like me, you used to sit and drink on a bar stool or your couch. It's a big world out there and you learn by doing, not by sitting around and thinking. You certainly don't learn by drinking. Physical activity can be the final proof that your brain needs to see that there's so much more to life than alcohol. Go get a rush, go get some new experiences and feel alive!!

The PASS Routine

I'm going to share with you a routine that I devised to kill restlessness. I've been using it for about a year now on a daily basis to alter my consciousness in a positive way.

It combines exercise, yoga, and meditation - and it takes less than 10 minutes.

Ex-drinkers have an abundance of restlessness. It can be made worse by anxiety and depression. Even when you're feeling good, your bones may scream at you for some kind of stimulation - anything! We need to calm our limbic systems.

Hence the PASS routine - as in "this too shall pass" - which is an immediate physical solution to existential anxiety and waves of restlessness:

Pushups - Do enough push-ups to get your heart rate up. I started with 35 and have worked my way up to 70. Push-up tips: Keep your hips aligned with your body as in a plank. Bring your chest as close to the floor as you can and lock out your elbows on the way up. If you can't do a full push-up, keep your knees on the floor and dip down just a few inches. Try to get lower each time, and you'll eventually achieve the full range of motion.

Air Squats - Now stand up and do the same number of air squats as you did for push-ups. You may find that putting your hands on your head helps you open your lungs and breathe more easily. Squat tips: Feet at least shoulder width, toes facing forward, back straight and butt out. Keep your shoulders square and chest out and drive through your heels on the way up. Keep your spine parallel with your shins throughout the movement.

Stretching - Now take a deep breath and work through the following five stretches at your own pace, feeling each one thoroughly before you move on to the next: Pigeon Pose, Downward Dog, Cobra Pose, Fire Log, and Front Splits. These will help you open your hips, which is where we store our stress and traumatic emotional memories. My two yogi friends gave me these stretches to maximize stress relief in the shortest period of time. Google the poses and try this progression for yourself - it works!!

Serenity - As you work through these stretches, you'll notice that your mind has cleared and you've moved into the present moment. Close your eyes, inhale deeply through your nose and hold your breath near your diaphragm. Exhale through your mouth, making a swish sound. Breathe in positive energy and exhale stress and negativity. Visualize your subconscious thoughts as a stream coming out of a spigot that you are gently shutting. Embrace the tension of each stretch. You are improving yourself, expanding your physical and psychological ranges of motion.

Observe how your state of mind changes after this progression. How do you feel compared to the way you felt 10 minutes ago? Do you feel more relaxed and more in control of the present moment? The initial intensity of the push-ups and air squats makes the yoga poses feel like well-earned relief. As the progression becomes automatic over time, you'll find that you look forward to doing it on a near-daily basis. Improvements in your push-up and squat form are merely positive byproducts of learning to assert dominance over your own mind in this way.

I first tried the PASS routine on a dark and rainy morning. I was anxious and it gave me a new sense of control. That was nearly a year ago. Since then, I've used it to put myself at ease before weddings and dates. Sometimes I'll jog to a scenic area near my home, enter a meditative trance as I work through the routine, and then walk back home. If you wake up feeling negative or unready to tackle the day, this routine will help you to break that thought pattern.

The hardest part is getting started. You're not working out to exhaustion; you're interrupting your train of thought so that you can achieve a better state of mind. Get out of bed, or off the couch, and put down your phone. Exercise is not a moral duty or a social obligation. It's your time to enhance your brain-body connection. It's a tool in your arsenal to seize control of small moments that might otherwise become enslaved by restlessness and stubborn thought patterns.

A Sample Exercise Plan

Strict diets and inflexible workout schedules are limiting. Over-scheduling causes unnecessary stress; subjecting your routine to occasional randomness strengthens your commitment. As with diet, the key is to substitute exercise that you enjoy for unhealthy activities that would otherwise dominate your schedule. You'll get into the habit of working out often and pushing your boundaries.

I start each morning with the PASS routine or 30 minutes of outdoor cardio. I lift weights for an hour in the afternoon or evening, three to five times per week. I'll do the PASS routine before stressful events or before doing something I don't want to do (like my taxes). Here's a sample plan that you can modify based on your schedule and preferences:

Monday: Morning - PASS routine. Evening - Lift, legs.

Tuesday: Morning - 30 minute jog. Evening - Lift, back and biceps.

Wednesday: Morning - PASS routine. Evening - Lift, chest, triceps.

Thursday: Morning - 30 minute bike ride. Evening - Rest.

Friday: Morning - PASS routine. Evening - Lift, focus on weak points.

Saturday: Morning - sparring session.

Sunday: Rest. Get outside for an adventure or an hour long walk.

Your workout schedule does not need to be more complicated than this. You're less likely to skip workouts if you write down your general plan in advance and commit to understanding the basics of good form. If you're interested in learning more about the specifics of lifting weights, I highly recommend Michael Matthews' Bigger Leaner Stronger (for men) or Thinner Leaner Stronger (for women).

Anyone can make time to exercise. Visualize your schedule and cut the unnecessary activities. From this moment onward, refuse to place a high value on low-value activities. Refuse to spend time with people who put you in a negative state, and reallocate wasted time to your own self-improvement. Every cell in your body will thank you in ways that you cannot imagine now.

CHAPTER 6

CREATE VIRTUOUS CYCLES

"When I'm doing all of the stuff that I'm supposed to do - when I'm writing a lot, I'm exercising a lot, I'm eating healthy - I have this momentum state that propagates success. "
-Joe Rogan

Did you ever notice that when you drank heavily, good habits never took hold for long? This is not a mystery. It's time to explode the destructive myth that drinking is somehow a pillar of a healthy lifestyle.

You can't start any day right when you're dealing with dehydration, headaches, or racing thoughts. Alcoholics associate these unpleasant experiences with the absence of alcohol, but they are inevitable byproducts of alcohol metabolism. The "hair of the dog" - that morning mimosa or five - makes you feel better temporarily, until you end up on your couch wondering what your day might have been like without it. Hmm, should I open a bottle of wine?

Every action produces an equal and opposite reaction. Every toxic buzz depletes the health of every cell in your body and produces a sickly low that forces you to address it. Drinking forces you to channel your energy into fixing malaise. Perhaps you rationalize away your goal for the day or you spend money on a convenient, greasy meal. Drinking really sucks because the kind of momentum it creates always reinforces vicious cycles, eventually culminating in never-ending drinking.

Have you ever had a vision of feeling happy, efficient, centered and pumped up for new experiences? This is an illusion that won't materialize unless you've quit drinking for good. The good news is that once you've quit, it can quickly become your new reality.

As I write this, I've just woken up at 8:37 AM on a Sunday morning without an alarm. Because I got eight hours of sleep, I feel rested and clear-minded. I jumped out of bed, savored the aroma of Colombian coffee, and banged out a PASS routine. I won't check my phone or the news until I finish this chapter. I'm looking forward to enjoying my cheat meal with family tonight. I might juice some vegetables and fruit in a few hours to hold me over until then. After four hours of work, I'll make sure I get outside for an hour.

I didn't spontaneously choose to be more disciplined than the next guy today. I don't have an abnormal amount of willpower. The years I spent waking up in a cold sweat and wasting entire days are proof that I haven't always chosen the best course of action in the moment.

You don't have the power to feel the way you want to in any given moment. But you do have the power to make small changes that add up to a superior lifestyle. If you stick with it, the ultimate benefit of this lifestyle is freedom from the glum sense of life that plagues people who obsess over T-shirt slogans about acceptance, forgiveness, surrender, etc. for the rest of their lives.

As you learned in the previous chapters, fixing your nutrient deficiencies, improving your diet, and becoming more active are not random luxuries. They are not simply optional tools for dominating alcohol. They are necessities if your goal is to feel relaxed and motivated as your default emotional settings. When you feel good on a daily basis, you accomplish small goals that can add up to something magnificent.

It's up to you to make the leap from reading the words in this book to taking real action. Once you do this, you will set into motion a series of virtuous cycles that are the exact opposite of the vicious cycle of alcohol addiction. Things that I could not achieve before I quit drinking - from small goals like waking up at a certain time and arriving early to meetings, to large goals like writing and reading on a daily basis - have materialized for me and become part of my reality. My current lifestyle seemed like a distant dream for many years.

...But Isn't Moderate Drinking a Healthy Habit?

Before we move on, let's explode some health myths about drinking.

You might have heard that drinking alcohol can prevent cancer. The research behind this claim is outdated. Countries are actively revising their alcohol intake guidelines, because wide-ranging research completed in 2016 has found that low levels of alcohol directly contribute to seven types of common cancers.

Drinking also does not prevent heart disease. Decades ago, researchers sought to explain the "French miracle," whereby French people with high fat diets managed to avoid heart disease, by pointing to their moderately high alcohol intake. New research has shown that this one-dimensional focus on dietary fat as the cause of heart disease is inaccurate. Genes and exercise play a role, but pasture-raised butter and meat, containing high levels of artery-unclogging CLA and Vitamin K2, can actually protect the heart.

Heavy drinking, on the other hand, causes weight gain and weakens the heart muscle over time, leading to heart failure. It turns out that on average, French people (and Italians and Spaniards) are good at maintaining moderate drinking levels without sliding into addiction. How could this be?

Alcohol has existed in Mediterranean culture for thousands of years - much longer than in, say, Irish, Russian, or Native American culture. Natural selection has removed much (though not all) of the susceptibility to alcohol addiction from the Mediterranean gene pool. The real "French miracle" - whereby the French drink, but tend to avoid addiction - probably has a genetic explanation.

With that said, the average French person drinks 120 bottles of wine per year. Drinking causes an estimated 50,000 premature deaths each year in that country. No one, addicted or not, is truly immune to the consequences of consuming a poison.

Building Lifestyle Momentum

Enough about the French. Let's return to discussing YOU.

You created negative momentum in your life when you drank. Alcohol simultaneously ruined your energy levels and condemned you to drinking even more as your condition deteriorated.

The opposite occurs as you tackle the puzzle of dominating alcohol. Discovering every missing piece that fits will propel you to a better "new normal" state. Over the next 30 days, you'll repair serious nutrient deficiencies that may have left you feeling anxious and depressed for months or even years. You'll feel more energy within days of changing your diet. Your exercise routine will lead to more ambitious goals outside of the gym. You'll soon fall asleep more easily at night and wake up feeling refreshed.

The greatest myth about fitness in the treatment industry is that its benefits are confined to the gym and the mirror. "You'll become a selfish fanatic who ignores your children!" This is pure horse shit and it is the favorite line of people who have self-image issues. Far from turning you into an insulated narcissist, higher energy levels will liberate you from a shortsighted and self-limiting focus on abstaining from alcohol. If you spend your life trying not to think of a pink elephant, your thoughts and dreams will be dominated by pink elephants. If you focus instead on becoming a lion, you'll forget all about pink elephants.

Beating Anxiety

"I have been through some terrible things in my life, some of which actually happened."

— Mark Twain

Earlier I wrote that you don't have the power to feel the way you want to in any given moment. Yet our moods and behavior are not entirely determined by our biochemical makeup. I will give you an example that illustrates this point.

James has been "sober" for a year and he has a severe magnesium deficiency. He also consumes too much sugar and rarely has the energy to exercise. His doctor has given him prescription medications for anxiety and insomnia. He accepts the idea that he has a debilitating disease that will always plague his behavior, and he believes that now that he has quit drinking (for today), his disease's permanent symptoms are alcohol cravings and random moments of panic. He says that he is okay, but meetings and books about spirituality do not help him to feel good.

Unable to take much pleasure in life, he falls into a deep depression. His posture deteriorates, his breathing becomes shallow and rapid, and he dwells on negative thoughts. The images, sounds, and sensations that run through his mind are the starkest possible representations of the outside world and his place within it.

The root of James' problems is biochemical. Prescription meds are band-aid approaches that temporarily relieve the symptoms of his magnesium deficiency, and his poor lifestyle habits make his condition worse. However, even if he started taking magnesium and getting fit, he would still need to address the negative physiological and mental patterns that his deficiency indirectly created.

Science is finally unlocking the ways in which good posture, deep breathing and meditation can reduce stress hormones and enhance cognition. Tools like these can bring James to the next level of happiness once he resolves his magnesium deficiency.

Learn to fix your posture when you find yourself slumping. Roll your shoulders back and keep your back muscles stacked over your hips. Allow your chest to protrude slightly and look straight ahead rather than down. Breathe in through your nose and deep into your lungs, near your diaphragm, and hold it there for a few seconds. Slowly release it through your mouth, and repeat several times. Your mind will clear and make way for thoughts of a higher quality: optimism, gratitude, motivation.

Envision yourself doing things that you will enjoy today and in the future. Visualizing your worst fears coming to fruition is a recipe for anxiety. In the short term, what you picture in your mind affects your mood. In the long-term, it creates your self-image, which is your subconscious mind's guide to your future actions. Have you ever sabotaged yourself and wondered why? Chances are good that your conscious goals - ambitious, bright, optimistic - conflicted with your self-image, which was dark and small.

About a year ago, after receiving an "urgent" piece of mail from the IRS, I felt sick to my stomach for an entire day. I realized that I'd been repeatedly and involuntarily picturing myself getting hauled off to jail. The scenario was so unlikely that it was patently absurd; still, it absolutely ruined my mood. It poked into my mind's eye when I was trying to get other things done. The pit in my stomach went away after I forced myself to open it, saw that I'd made a mistake the previous year, and mailed a check in. Avoiding responsibilities I didn't like was a habit I'd formed in my drinking days.

Isn't problem resolution just common sense? Not in my case. It took repeated effort to make dealing with urgent things a habit. Now that decisive action is a habit, 99% of my problems disappear very quickly. Procrastination always drains more willpower than action.

A small adjustment in your lifestyle can become the difference that makes a much bigger difference.

New Habits and Rituals

My girlfriend asked me, "Did you sleep good?" I said, "No, I made a few mistakes."

— Steven Wright

Even when I was physically addicted to alcohol and unable to safely quit on my own, there were certain cues that alerted me that it was time to drink. Getting home from work after a long day and sitting down on my couch felt strange unless I had a drink in my hand. Going to a party and hearing a noisy crowd made me salivate for alcohol. Near the end of my addiction, merely having a negative thought - one that I had subconsciously generated, and which I refused to consciously challenge - seemed to make my head spin until I had a drink.

Your new lifestyle will revolve around an entirely new set of cues and behaviors. Not all of them will be conscious, so it's up to you to make sure that they promote virtuous cycles rather than vicious ones. As you continue to practice your new habits and rituals, they will become automatic.

Below are some lifestyle habits that I've developed and which you might find helpful. These are merely suggestions:

- **Halt your thought patterns**. Give yourself a 15 minute meditation time-out each day with comfortable pillows, a salt lamp, and a Youtube video (search for binaural or theta beats)

- **Try progressive relaxation**. Sequentially and consciously relax every part of your body from head to toe - your eyes, cheeks, jaw, neck, spine, arms, hands, fingers, etc. - all the way down to your toes.

- **Choose one meditation mantra**. In time, saying your mantra will bring relaxation and focus in any setting, because your brain will associate it with these states.

- **Read until you fall asleep at night**. You'll kill three birds with one stone: you'll tire your eyes before sleeping, alter your consciousness naturally, and infuse your subconscious mind with fresh thoughts.

- **Avoid caffeine after noon**. It takes 10 hours for caffeine to leave your system.

- **Avoid TV and web surfing in the morning**. These things pollute your subconscious mind with irrelevant worries, ruining clarity of thought.

- **Arrive 10 minutes early for everything**. Train your brain to stop freaking out over being late for meetings and important appointments.

- **Set one realistic goal each morning**. In a year's time, you will be at least 365 steps further along than you are now

- **Think of 3 things you're grateful for each morning**. This strategy will reduce any situational anxiety or depression that you may be experiencing.

- **Keep an idea journal**. Become conscious of your thought patterns and excited about goals you want to accomplish in the future

- **Become an unshakeable optimist**. Don't get captured by negativity. Remind yourself to experience each moment fully instead of ruminating about things you don't like and can't control.

At first glance, these tips might seem small and inconsequential. Remember that the greatest transformations begin with the smallest changes.

It's Not All Willpower and Sacrifice

Isn't freedom your ultimate goal? You want freedom from drinking and thoughts about drinking. You want to be liberated from unhealthy cycles that dominate your life. You want to find meaning in life that has nothing to do with alcohol or that infamous negative: abstinence. You cannot choose to recover instantaneously and feel amazing in any given moment (however, as we will see, you have more power in the present moment than you think). You can choose to make small changes in your daily habits that add up to a superior lifestyle.

None of this requires superhuman willpower, discipline, and sacrifice. Just as a powerlifter no longer requires all of his energy to lift 200 pounds, so you will not always need to summon all of your willpower to avoid alcohol and pursue your vision of happiness. As you build your physical and mental muscles, discipline will become your natural choice.

You're going somewhere, and you should savor every moment along the way. You won't get any of these moments back. Your brain is rewiring with every tick of the clock, allowing you to transform into the person you always knew you could be. Stand up straight, take a deep breath, and close your eyes. Give yourself permission to feel happy right now.

CHAPTER 7

MASTER YOUR MIND

"Learning that the impossible is possible augments our ability to see ourselves doing the impossible, which triggers a systemic change in the body and the brain, which closes the gap between fantasy and reality."
-Steven Kotler

If you have begun to implement the advice in this book, congratulations on your courage. You will soon be ready to climb up the cliff above the fjord and triumphantly yell once and for all, DRINKING SUCKS!!! You will then be free to focus on things that are much more important than poison.

Exactly two years after I had my last drink - or my last 25 drinks - I walked up the steps into my new place. The neighbors had heard that I was moving in and they'd decided to buy me a housewarming gift. The guy next door smiled as he warmly presented me with a bottle of Pinot Noir. I stopped for a second and considered the date and the irony. Then I thanked him, chuckled to myself and sent my roommate a text: "The neighbors got us a bottle of wine. It's all yours!" Then I forgot all about it. I think that he shared the bottle with a date in our living room.

I was able to forget about the bottle of wine because I had

reframed my perception of alcohol. I had trained myself to stop seeing wine as a magical and delicious formula for instant gratification. At one point, I would have considered this reaction to be impossible. By choice, I began to see it as rotten headache juice that smelled like potpourri; a dehydrating beverage that I used to stupidly equate with being social and relaxed before I realized that one can be cool, calm and upbeat without any help from artificial highs.

Seeing that bottle of Pinot made me feel lucky that I had figured out the secrets of mental mastery. I knew how to feel things that other people needed wine to feel. Carrying the bottle into the house for my roommate, I felt proud and silently emotional.

Ironically, yet by intention, I had turned wine bottles into anchors that immediately evoked feelings of triumph and self-confidence. In this chapter I will show you how to do the same thing. Alcohol does not need to trigger conflicted emotions - shame, warmth, guilt, desire, cognitive dissonance, frantic phone calls…You do not need to condemn your mind to a pendulum of temptation and redemption.

As human beings, we only follow courses of action that have perceived benefits. This is a fundamental fact of human nature. We instinctively avoid courses of action with no perceived benefits, or which only hold perceived dangers. Our perceptions tend to operate on a subconscious level, but this does not mean that they are beyond our control. We can change them by constructing new frames, which are the essential facts and emotions that we associate with a particular concept. We can change our emotions by establishing new anchors, which are sensations or thoughts that automatically trigger a certain state of mind in any given moment.

Your subconscious mind at some point framed alcohol as a precursor to the release of feel-good chemicals. Once you repair your brain, your conscious mind can reprogram your subconscious mind rather quickly. You have already introduced exercise and other virtuous cycles as new sources of feel-good chemicals. The final step is twofold: first, to destroy your associations between alcohol and desirable states of mind - and second, to mentally immunize yourself from drinking at social scenes where alcohol is present.

The techniques in this chapter will only help once you have quit drinking and started to repair your system. Active addiction is a biochemical puzzle; seeing that drinking sucks and effortlessly avoiding it, once you're free, is a mindset. DRINKING SUCKS may sound light-hearted, even juvenile, but it is a very powerful mindset.

Your Brain & Your Mind

At the risk of sounding repetitive, I want to answer an objection: If addiction is a physical brain condition, whose resolution requires biochemical repair, then what does the mind have to do with it?

For our purposes here, let's define your brain as a hunk of gray matter that is concerned primarily with your survival. Your mind transcends physical matter; it is composed of your thoughts, values, and goals. You can develop the power to choose between automatic impulses provided by your brain - which, in the case of alcohol addiction, are false and dangerous - and freely chosen messages that you create through conscious thought. Once your brain is healthy enough to permit conscious thought to overrule subconscious impulses, you can begin to use your mind to physically rewire your brain.

This is why biochemical repair is a prerequisite for mastering your mind. In a state of severe active addiction, the brain enslaves the mind, activating primitive panic responses to ensure continued alcohol consumption. The advice in this chapter will only be relevant once you have provided your brain with everything it needs to achieve chemical balance.

Can My Mind Really Rewire My Brain?

In their enlightening book, *You Are Not Your Brain*, psychiatrists Jeffrey Schwartz and Rebecca Gladding offer a four step treatment plan for eliminating bad behaviors that emanate from deceptive brain messages. I will briefly summarize them as follows:

- **Relabel** deceptive brain messages
- **Reframe** the meaning of these messages
- **Refocus** on something better than these messages
- **Revalue** these messages so that they become unworthy of consideration

When a group of unmedicated OCD patients used these four steps for ten weeks, brain scans found that the part of their brains responsible for OCD symptoms had decreased in size. Symptoms diminished significantly and the results were comparable to those who had been medicated. Yes, your conscious mind can help to physically rewire your brain.

Schwartz and Gladding clarify that these steps "can help anyone with excessive nervousness, worry and anxiety, tension, depression, anger, substance abuse, [and] other addictions." I would add that physical fitness is a powerful method of refocusing our attention away from our society's cult-like worship of alcoholic destruction.

The authors of this book make clear that these four steps are often necessary, but not sufficient, to beat habits that are deeply ingrained in the brain. Chemical addictions and conditions like OCD exist on spectrums. These steps would not have kept me away from the bottle at the height of my addiction, but they're nearly identical to the methods I used to avoid relapse after I'd achieved a baseline level of brain chemistry balance.

"Drinking Sucks" is the Ultimate Reframe

The way you think influences the way you feel. What are the essential facts about drinking in your own mind? Do you still see it through a rose-colored lens? Even if you know that drinking is a net negative for your life, do you still associate it with feelings of freedom, joy, or nostalgia? If you do, let me help you fix this.

The truth is that you can see alcohol as a forbidden fruit or as an unnecessary toxin disguised by clever marketing. You can associate alcohol with the fleeting highs it once gave you, or you can associate it with the lows. You can perceive your teetotaling at social events as unfair punishment, or you can see it as an opportunity to express your personality and develop your newfound strengths.

Below are some of the ways in which I've reframed my perception of drinking. I can think of many personal experiences that confirm my new beliefs. For each one, several vivid events from my past stand out in my mind as the ultimate proof. Do the same thing with your own experiences. Tie these assertions together with your own subjective reality and repeat them to yourself several times. Reflect on this list as often as you need to until you create a new mental frame for alcohol.

- ~~Drinking gives me a nice buzz~~. **Drinking makes me woozy.**

- ~~All the cool people drink~~. **Drinking makes awkward people louder.**

- ~~Alcohol is a safe drug~~. **Alcohol is a dirty drug with bad side effects.**

- ~~Drinking helps me get to sleep~~. **Drinking screws up my sleep cycles.**

- ~~Alcohol has health benefits~~. **Alcohol screws up my health.**

- ~~Drinking is sexy~~. **Drinking screws up my physique.**

- ~~Drinking makes me funny~~. **Drinking makes me obnoxious.**

- ~~Drinking makes me confident.~~ **Drinking inevitably creates anxiety.**

- ~~Drinking makes me a badass.~~ **Not being a sheep makes me a badass.**

It's amazing that more people who have quit drinking haven't concluded that drinking sucks.

Equate drinking with bodily destruction, not bliss: "This activity - this dirty drug - offers me nothing." I can remember feeling woozy and bad after drinking too much, I can remember when I first realized that alcohol is the opiate of the masses - a social crutch even for people who aren't physically addicted to it. I can remember having terrible workouts while withdrawing and waking up in the middle of the night feeling a cold sweat and a sense of impending doom. All of the reframes above tie drinking to debunked misconceptions that I used to believe - or to undesirable physical states that I've physically felt.

Focus on destroying false assumptions about how drinking will cause you to act or feel, but avoid linking booze to depressing emotions or long causal chains. For example, "Alcohol makes my family hate me" may not be effective. It's more likely to make you feel resentful or depressed than create a physical aversion to alcohol in any given moment. The goal is to dislike alcohol at first glance, not to dislike yourself after opening old emotional wounds.

"Alcohol dehydrates my skin" can be an effective reframe. (I read somewhere that J Lo doesn't drink, and this was the reason she gave for abstaining.) This kind of reframe cancels out the sexy image created by the media, and is more likely to make you feel proud of your physical progress than depressed about your past. "Alcohol makes classy people sloppy" is also a good one, since it destroys the carefully manufactured image of the sophisticated drinker.

Add your own reframes in the spaces below or on a notepad.

Make sure you cross out your old assumptions (as I did above) and actively associate your new assumptions with your own experiences that confirm their validity in your mind.

This exercise actually works if you do it. If you went ahead with the exercise, congratulations on making your life much easier going forward.

Now let's move on and reframe the taste of alcohol. Let's be honest: beer is foul yeast soda. You were supremely disappointed the first time you tasted it in high school, even if you got hooked on its temporary effects. Wine drinking is bullshit entertainment for people who want to look sophisticated by getting expensively drunk. Hard apple cider tastes exactly like sparkling apple cider with added alcohol. Hard liquor is reminiscent of paint thinner and gasoline. People build a taste tolerance to these things, but they're still amazed when they can find "oaky notes" in otherwise caustic-smelling whiskies. What's amazing is that they've managed to numb themselves to the foul taste in the first place. The more you drink, the "better" it tastes - because ethanol is an anesthetic that numbs your taste.

My dad quit drinking to help me see that there's more to life (he never had a problem with alcohol). He then went to a wine tasting party and was disgusted by the taste of the same wines that he used to enjoy. To this day, he rarely drinks because he sees that our culture has built a series of illusions around alcohol. The frames through which even non-alcoholics see alcohol simply make little sense to him. He sees clearly that a drink creates about 10 minutes of energy, followed by tiredness and disorientation that can be exchanged for (and compounded by) another drink - and if he has enough of these, he will feel fuzzy. Even for a so-called normal drinker, this is a bad tradeoff. Instead of sipping beer on the couch during football games, he now does a pushup every time his team scores a point. All of his friends, some of whom are heavy drinkers, know that he no longer drinks - and none of them care.

You don't have to swear off events and parties to see our culture of heavy drinking for what it is: a cult of silent destruction. You're not missing out. At one time you were part of it, and you saw that it's not all it's cracked up to be. Rise above it.

I sense an objection: Are we merely telling ourselves useful lies about alcohol? The answer to this question is absolutely not! We are finally telling ourselves the truth about a substance that has damaged our health and our lives. It is downright ILLOGICAL to deny the harm that drinking brings to your body and mind right away. Yet this kind of denial is what addiction does to us. We are finally reversing that denial once and for all.

You already know that drinking takes your vital life force out of you in many different ways. You have the power to choose a conscious life over mindless destruction.

Creating New Anchors

Since drinking is so undesirable, you can turn alcohol symbols into a source of strength. This is how you transcend addiction instead of remaining in the maze with your hands over your eyes forever.

Let me introduce anchors by giving you two examples that have nothing to do with alcohol. The smell of fish has physically repulsed my mom for as long as I can remember. She associated it with her father making her gut fish as a child. A few years ago on a trip to Sicily, she decided to give fish another try. She now orders it fairly often. At some point along the road, she must have replaced her old anchor (the smell of fish) with a newer, more powerful one that allowed her to change her eating behavior.

The second example I'll give you is my reaction to hearing depressing music in grocery stores. For some reason, large chains love playing morose songs that my ex-girlfriends played constantly. Hearing them in a store makes me annoyed at the store for reminding me of failed relationships. I'm an emotionally stable person, but these particular songs are anchors for undesirable states of mind. If I'm ever in charge of a grocery chain, the first thing I'll do is cut the sad songs and boost sales.

As with reframing, I came across the concept of anchors after learning about neuro-linguistic programming (NLP). You can create new anchors just as you can construct new frames. The idea is to associate a word, image, sound, or other sensation with a desirable mental state like joy, relaxation, or motivation. The key is consciously, repetitively producing the state of mind you desire in the presence of the given anchor. Once the anchor is established in your subconscious mind, repeating the word, seeing the image, hearing the sound, or feeling the sensation will automatically trigger that state of mind.

I have a meditation mantra that automatically brings me relaxation and focus when I'm on the verge of losing my cool about something. It works because I've been using this mantra for years and my mind automatically associates it with relaxation. I've used it to thwart angry meltdowns and bring my pulse down to help me fall asleep.

I mentioned earlier that I had managed to turn wine bottles into anchors for feelings of self-confidence. This does not mean that I go looking for wine bottles when I want to feel good about myself. While meditating two years ago, I began working myself into an intensely euphoric state over my transformation since quitting alcohol, and then I began picturing wine bottles, beer bottles, crowded parties and other scenes that others might associate with "relapse." I envisioned myself confronting these concepts effortlessly, thoroughly enjoying the company of friends and family without the slightest inclination to drink. Then I associated this experience with "greatness" - and not of the drinking variety.

Scenes in which others are drinking now remind me that my mission in life is greatness, not alcoholic intoxication. My reaction to seeing other people drinking is a sense of triumph over my past. This strategy has allowed me to enjoy countless social events and a number of weddings since I quit drinking. These days, I barely notice the alcohol, and I feel calm and confident by default.

The trick is to reframe drinking as inherently undesirable, even gross, while turning mental images of social scenes, alcohol bottles, bar signs, and billboard beer advertisements into anchors that empower you. Why not make your enemies work for you? You won't escape them unless you decide to move to a desert island.

The idea of feeling victorious - or even just not wanting to drink - at the sight of a wine bottle is unheard of in the treatment industry. We are told to go to lengths to avoid alcohol and to fear it so much that merely seeing it will require us to call "sober buddies." We are conditioned to turn our mental image of alcohol into an anchor for feelings of panic and powerlessness. The proposed solution for this state - to defy our desires and submit to others - leads to resentment. This is a disaster, especially if our subconscious minds still frame alcohol as a viable solution for feelings of panic, powerlessness, and resentment.

Fragile Addict or Antifragile Warrior?

I don't see people with past addictions as inherently fragile or powerless. Of course, you can choose to frame yourself in this way. And you can choose to weaken your body and your mind very quickly if you randomly decide to start hammering drinks. But our behavior is not random. It is programmed into our brains by our biochemistry and our subconscious assumptions. We can influence both of these things.

Instead of seeing yourself as a perpetually fragile "addict in recovery," seek to become antifragile, which is a concept invented by Nassim Taleb. This term means the ability to thrive from uncertainty, disorder, chaos. Not to merely absorb shocks, but to become better, stronger, and happier because of them. No one ever achieved happiness in the absence of risk and uncertainty. Learn to make reality work for you rather than against you.

If you can turn the sight of wine bottles into anchors that reaffirm your identity as a proud nondrinker, you are the very definition of antifragile.

A few years ago, a friend called me up out of the blue. He and I had always been in competition with each other - in school, in sports, and then in our careers. He knew that I had quit the corporate world and temporarily withdrawn into my own bubble to battle my own demons. Instead of gloating, he said this: "You're unstoppable now. You know pain better than any of us, and I bet nothing scares you anymore." I thought about this for a second. I had narrowly escaped drinking myself to death, and nothing mattered to me anymore except my strongest relationships and my mission in life. Near-disaster had vastly simplified my life, and my appreciation for life was reborn. There was no place for petty fear anymore. My friend was right.

What doesn't kill you will make you stronger. Control those obstacles that used to control you. Turning them into crippling phobias is never the answer. Be patient - it may take some time to build up your own power and resourcefulness. You're a warrior on a mission, not a kite in the wind.

CHAPTER 8

GET HIGH ON LIFE

"Don't ask what the world needs. Ask what makes you come alive.
Because what the world needs most is more people who have come
alive."
-Howard Thurman

Long before I realized that drinking sucks, I figured that it was
impossible to feel high on life without drinking. Nondrinkers who
said they were high on life just had to be faking it. They couldn't
possibly feel as warm, euphoric, sociable, and connected to the
universe as I did with a drink in my hand. Every drink picked me up,
for about 10 minutes at a time, even though I was out of shape, felt
sick until I drank, and had no objective progress in my life to
celebrate.

Connected to the universe?

The panicked, morose and lonely aftermath of drinking heavily
was the trade-off for feeling good sometimes, right? What a trap this
reality is - what a hilarious trap - and how funny it seemed to me
when I was temporarily high on alcohol.

I would sometimes sit at a bar alone, with a conflicted smirk on
my face, chuckling about my predicament. No one could understand,
but everyone drinks, right?

It turns out that the warm euphoria, that vividly positive experience that gradually fades as addiction progresses, has nothing to do with alcohol at all. It is created by chemicals that are already in our own brains, and for heavy drinkers, alcohol simply monopolizes them. If you've quit drinking forever, your most intense euphoria lies in the future, not the past. Especially if you've gotten to the point where the negative aftermath of drinking eclipses the illusion of happiness.

The truth that eluded me when I drank is that many people who don't drink have enviable life experiences. They seek and find excitement, adventure, fulfillment, endorphin rushes, spiritual epiphanies, physical ecstasy - all without ever participating in society's groupthink-worship of toxic euphoria followed by hangovers. In fact, they have an advantage precisely because they don't drink.

Let's assume that most people lack the biochemistry to become addicted to alcohol as quickly as we did. Even if this is true, many of them still feel the need to escape from their lives over and over again. Alcohol is the opiate of the masses, addicted or not. The masses do not tend to align their feel-good chemicals with a sense of fulfillment. The vast majority of people fail to create lives that they don't want to escape from. Isn't this more tragic than your decision not to drink?

You might point out that artificial highs can enhance the experiences of people who do not want to escape their lives. But I have yet to find a substance that gives a high without a corresponding low. If it exists, I'm not necessarily opposed to it. Marijuana, Kratom, and Phenibut are all safer than alcohol, and we see people switching to these as alcohol's toxic effects become better understood. Yet these substances can also produce lows, and a few of them can lead to milder but very real addictions.

I don't see the point of living in fear that second-hand marijuana smoke from my neighbor's balcony could send me back into an alcoholic relapse. I don't even refer to myself as sober. I've simply learned that I can experience euphoria on my own. And I'll never forget how much drinking sucks!

The Benefits of Being Different

Refusing to participate in society's mindless obsession with booze is not a handicap. The people with the worst handicaps are those who think that getting wasted every weekend has no consequences. If you feel like death for 50 Saturday mornings out of every year, you're dampening your potential in life, to put it mildly.

And if you avoid this common but mindless state of existence, then you have discovered a strength, not a weakness. Being different is not a curse. Let me draw an analogy: I've gone through life with 50% hearing impairment in both ears. I do not wear hearing aids. Accepting that I'm different from other people was the first step in allowing me to develop strengths that I might have otherwise neglected. I spent more time reading books and cultivating a visual perspective of the world. I learned to read lips. I can determine what other people are saying from across a crowded room.

If I could turn my hearing loss into a net positive, it wasn't much of a stretch to imagine that I could do the same thing with being a nondrinker. You can free your mental and physical resources in ways that most drinkers cannot imagine. Reframing alcohol is just a first step in realizing the benefits of being different.

"Work Hard, Play Hard"

This shopworn phrase, which is often taken to mean, "Endure boring work, then drink yourself stupid" - is one of the biggest canards our society has ever invented. The happiest people do not turn work and play into enemies that fight to death in a zero-sum game. They find creative ways to make work and play mutually reinforce each other, often seamlessly blending them together.

The happiest people who still drink typically drink much less than I'd assumed. They go to parties to enjoy other people's company. It's almost as if they know that alcohol is a trap, and they're secretly laughing while they watch the same morons get hammered each time. I once watched an immensely successful woman hold the same glass of wine for an hour at a company party, and then put it down halfway through without even thinking about it. She hadn't taken a sip and seemed to be the definition of confident, laid back, and high on life. On the other hand, I do not know of any heavy drinkers who do not battle person demons - for whom alcohol takes less out of them than they take out of alcohol, to paraphrase the heavy-drinking and heroic, yet chronically depressed, Winston Churchill.

Think about it this way: You can actually do those things that drunk people on barstools fantasize about and never turn into reality. The key to keeping what you want - a happy, fulfilling, exciting life - is to enable yourself to take pride in your individuality and thoroughly enjoy the less-traveled path that you're on.

Sober Raves?!

I want to digress for moment here, because I came across something that is very telling about our culture's relationship with alcohol, on several levels.

Although raves were never part of my lifestyle, I was amused and happy to read the other day that "sober raves" are now a thing. With health consciousness going mainstream in our culture, a small but still surprising number of people have concluded that they can keep their celebratory sense of life intact - and their dance parties going - without destroying their bodies in the process. Green juices and coffees are the norm at these morning dance parties, which are cropping up in major cities across America. Even if these events don't appeal to you, there's no question that the partygoers are clearly high on life.

But what stood out to me most about the articles I read was the level of vitriol in the comment section, followed by the incredulous reactions by normal commenters to such vitriol. Could alcohol be so ingrained in our culture that writing a story about sober raves brings some drinkers to the brink of an identity crisis?

To the chagrin of those booze-obsessed (or hangover-ridden) commenters, the sober rave-goers are demonstrating that alcohol is merely a cleverly marketed and totally unnecessary toxin. They are not celebrating merely the absence of alcohol, but the vastness and worthiness of the universe beyond it.

If the word "sober rave" strikes you as an oxymoron, that's because it is. It's unfortunate that the only adjective we have to describe nondrinkers is "sober." This word means abstinence from alcohol, but it is commonly taken to mean abstinence from fun. Merriam-Webster includes in its list of definitions: "marked by temperance," "subdued in tone or color," and "showing no excessive or extreme qualities." In other words, boring. Sober does not fairly express the sentiment of people who think of their lives as parties without alcohol.

Some of the resistance to quitting drinking has nothing to do with alcohol and much to do with the boring word that we use to describe nondrinkers. People who have more interesting things to do than drink are rarely boring. For a time I described myself as sober, but I have moved away from it because it does not accurately describe my sense of life.

Internal Fire vs Escape

Because you no longer drink, you have a unique opportunity to create a life that contains, throughout its course, the very highs that many people know only as "escape." When I hear someone say that he or she needs escape, I wonder what that person is running from.

I'm not talking about vacations or holiday escapes. I'm referring to a perpetual desire to escape reality, which builds up over time, because life seems dull instead of fulfilling.

The antidote to the need for continual escape is internal fire, which is what drives you toward your purpose and imbues all other natural highs with significance. If you have internal fire, then every other natural high - physical feats, jet skiing, road trips with friends, bonfires on foreign beaches, making impressions on new people as your best possible self - becomes a memorable experience that is congruent with your overall sense of life. The moments you live for should not be guilty distractions that you later justify with reference to groupthink.

A perpetual desire to escape - to truly escape from reality, not to achieve a healthy and well-earned release - is the consequence of having no internal fire.

When I quit drinking, I had no internal fire to speak of. But I knew that I lacked it, and I found through trial and error that there are two keys to creating it. The first is to transfer physical energy, created by your workouts, into your pursuits outside of the gym. The second is to attach the simple highs that you already enjoy - for example, coffee, music, and friendship - with productive pursuits that you know will bring long-term happiness.

The transferring of physical energy into other goals is similar to Napoleon Hill's concept of the transmutation of sexual energy. Hill theorized that great achievers had figured out how to turn their libido into a source of productive power, by redirecting it toward the pursuit of great things. Within a few weeks of workouts as a nondrinker, you'll find that you have more energy than you know what to do with (as long as you repair your brain with nutrients). Your body is adapting to your workouts by invigorating your body and mind. Don't waste your post-workout highs feeling great in front of the TV. Write down any and all ideas, read books that can transform your life, and get started on building the life that you deserve. Your internal fire begins as a small spark. It is not an unsustainable "pink cloud." Once you get it raging, it will become a damn near limitless source of motivation.

If you can associate natural highs with productive activities, you can reduce the amount of discipline it takes to pursue your happiness. I'll give you a few of examples from my life. I associate coffee in the morning with writing. Every morning is a good morning because I'm drinking coffee and writing. I associate my favorite music with great workouts. Certain songs are natural anchors that create physical energy. I bond with certain friends while working out and discuss business plans with others. There is no conflict between happiness and productivity.

I'm not saying that you should either be working or working out all the time. There's inherent value in joking around with friends and savoring the small moments. Surrounding yourself with great people is an end in itself, and our relationships with other people are often the most important things in our lives. The point is to harness your internal fire to achieve congruence between the things that bring you pleasure and the direction that you want your life to move toward.

When you develop internal fire, other people will be drawn to you like magnets. Interpersonal and tribal bonds are sources of pleasure in themselves. We evolved as social animals; our need to share our experiences with others is a hardwired trait. Choose your friends carefully. The more you focus on your own self-improvement, the more freedom you will have to associate with the kinds of people who can help you feel better than alcohol ever could.

End the tug of war between pleasure and purpose. A three week vacation to the Maldives can be congruent with your purpose in life. It might be a well-earned release, just as a workout is your endorphin release. But it is not an escape from your life. When you do not have a dull life to run away from, you will not need an escape.

How to Feel High on Life

I won't sugar coat reality. Some days will always be better than others. Sometimes you'll stub your toe twice on the way to the bathroom in the morning. You may have to cut your workout short because you'll spend 10 minutes untangling your earbuds, which turn out to be broken. You might take a long walk and end up getting bitten by a deer. Life can be crazy.

Below are a few ways that have helped me feel high on life most of the time. In time, the 15% of the time that you don't feel high on life will serve an important purpose. It will remind you that the 85% is pretty awesome.

- **Endorphins + Oxytocin = Euphoria**. In other words: Convince at least one friend to be your workout buddy.

- **Get 7-9 hours of sleep every night**. The amount of sleep you get directly affects your energy, attitude and resilience the next day.

- **Dress better than you have to**. When it's clear that you respect yourself, other people will follow your lead. You control the way others treat you. Dress well before hitting the grocery store.

- **Cultivate real, one-on-one friendships**. The loneliest people in the world are those who get drunk with strangers and have no one to talk to the next morning. You'll never feel left out of anything if you know who your real friends are.

- **Engage strangers in a small way every day**. Hold doors, ask store clerks how their days are going, leave outsized tips for good service. Practice eliciting positivity and cooperation from other people.

- **Write down your next adventure plans now**. The world is a big place and you deserve to see it. Put all of the money you used to spend on alcohol each week into a future travel account.

- **Laugh at everything that isn't an actual tragedy**. The small stuff never matters; only your response to it does. There's humor in pretty much everything, so find it and relish it.

- **Think to yourself, "this is awesome" when you feel good**. It could be the rush of a personal best in the gym, a rooftop view with a date, feeling clear and confident in situations that used to trigger discomfort, or savoring a great steak that you can actually taste and which you'll remember vividly.

- **Remember you live in a vast and exhilarating cosmos**. I've lost people I loved, I've been fired from jobs, and I've been hurt in relationships. It doesn't matter, because we're all lucky specks of dust that exist for a nanosecond of cosmic time. Let go and enjoy the ride.

- **Get into a steam room or sauna and then take a cold shower**. You'll release endorphins, improve your health, and feel insanely good. I try to do this after every workout.

Here's another tip: Listen to standup comedy while you're doing dull chores (dishes, laundry). I've listened to Louis CK's old routines countless times. Find the humor in things that make you miserable and frustrated. If you once used alcohol to get you through mundane chores, you'll begin to associate them with existential hilarity - or at least your favorite comedian. You might even start looking forward to doing them.

Find Better Ways to Alter Your Consciousness

Let me first say that I've never tried hard drugs because I always intuitively sensed that I would become addicted to them. But I have discovered that I enjoy altering my consciousness - and that it is possible to do so without ruining myself with toxic, addictive, life-draining substances.

Just as human beings evolved as social animals, so we evolved to alter our consciousness. No one is doomed to simply sit and reflect on the often cold, bland, damp here-and-now. We feel what we focus on and we can always improve reality. Every time we DO anything, we alter our consciousness. Eating, sleeping, exercising, traveling - these are natural ways in which we alter our consciousness all the time.

Our species latched onto drinking because it alters our state of mind quickly and temporarily. You will discover that there are much better ways to transcend mundane routines that aren't circular traps with nasty side effects. Once your body and mind heal, you'll have an epiphany: relaxed bliss is really only possible without drinking.

Walk slowly through a cathedral at dusk. Join a group of people dancing around a bonfire. Go on a spirit quest deep into the woods and meditate for three hours in a cave. Free your spirit and open your mind. Discover new herbs and create new rituals. Read books about subjects that arouse your curiosity. The quest for knowledge is a drug in itself.

Don't think that you have to gather all of the answers. The deepest recesses of our brains are intertwined with our pleasure pathways and they are not always accessible by reason. You will find surprising new ways to heighten the quality of your experience on earth.

You'll instinctively know if you're about to cross a line that can damage your life. You learn a lot about yourself when you successfully quit drinking. Contrary to conventional wisdom, you will become wiser and more careful. You will not become mindlessly "cross-addicted" to every activity that feels good.

The alcoholic label does not need to follow you around and haunt you forever. Alcoholism is only an omnipresent specter if you picture it that way. Likewise, other people's stringent definitions of sobriety do not need to mean anything to you. Don't let anyone else define or control you in order to make sense of their own lives.

CHAPTER 9

LIVE YOUR PURPOSE

"He who has a why to live can bear almost any how."
-Friedrich Nietzsche

To transcend drinking culture, you need a sacred sense of purpose. This will be your barrier against mindless groupthink. Living your purpose, being true to yourself, is the most difficult and rewarding challenge of all.

We live in a society plagued by a crisis of self-worth. Self-improvement blogs have sprung up and helped millions of people transform their lives. The most common piece of advice is to start with your body. Eat better food, work out more, and let yourself recharge. Learn to become confident and assertive. If you hate your job, find alternative work instead of letting your resentment fester. Focus on things you can control instead of dwelling on things you cannot control. Over time, your sphere of control will widen.

Fitness is a powerful weapon against sliding back into addiction because it is something we can control almost immediately. You can get yourself to the gym and feel proud of it. You can feel your energy levels improve within days of starting a solid routine and changing your diet. Igniting this virtuous cycle will increase your sense of possibility in life, along with your level of self-worth, which will become an additional barrier to relapse. You can turn independent self-improvement into an open, free spirited way of life.

For those of us with past addictions, surrendering without self-improvement is like extinguishing a house fire and refusing to build another home. You could use the possibility of another fire as an excuse to live in the ashes of the last one. You could find a support group filled with people who talk about fires constantly. In the immediate aftermath of tragedy, it might be reassuring to talk to nice people who have made peace with the idea that their living situations will be perpetually shabby. But if you want to build a mansion in the place of your old home, you can't afford to be stagnant. Channel your time and energy toward fulfilling your vision.

Does anguish have utility beyond allowing us to make peace with powerlessness? It's all in the way you frame it. You can use your past, and all of the pain you've endured, as an excuse to settle for mediocrity - or you can use it as steroids for your spirit. If you've writhed in the pits of alcoholic hell and moved on without becoming emotionally crippled, you're a miracle. One objective down, so what's next? My proudest moments have always come from defying the odds, especially when they are stacked against me.

Envisioning Your Purpose

Once alcohol becomes a moot substance, you'll crowd out alcoholic thoughts with better ones. "Will I drink today?" will simply stop occurring to you, even when you happen to be surrounded by alcohol. You might wake up one day and realize that it's been weeks or months since you thought about drinking. Congratulate yourself as you move on to the bigger, grander questions in life.

Resurrecting your brain, body and mind will free you to ask yourself: Where should I channel all of this new energy? How can I leverage my lifestyle, and my ever-increasing momentum, to help others and myself? How can I do this on the greatest scale and with the most magnitude?

It's okay if you don't know the answers to these questions yet. Allow yourself to slowly cultivate a renewed sense of mission. I read this line somewhere, and it has become one of my favorite mantras, even though I cannot remember who said it: Don't worry and don't hurry.

Make lists of things that you might have been born to accomplish. Reflect on your childhood obsessions and your innate talents. The quest to find your unique purpose in life can be a mission in itself. Unlike the quest to abstain from drinking, it is a positive goal rather than a negative one.

Addiction is a biochemical disorder, but finding your life's mission is a crucial piece of the addiction puzzle. I think of it as the glass frame that you use to hang the puzzle on your wall once and for all. If your frame is strong, it will keep the pieces of the puzzle from ever coming apart again. If you take care of your frame, it will permanently keep these pieces in perspective for you. You no longer live to drink; you live to be the person you want to be.

Fitness as a Launchpad

Even a year after I quit drinking, my mission in life was not obvious to me. I seemed to have some diverse talents that formed an incoherent whole, and I had no idea how to monetize them or put them to use helping other people. It would have been easy to throw up my hands and become a nihilist. In retrospect, I'm grateful that I channeled my sense of mission into the gym until I developed a more complete perspective on my life.

Fitness is not just a physical condition. It is the ability to overcome obstacles and adapt to whatever life throws at you. "Survival of the fittest" makes clear that fitness means competence.

Positive self-image - brought about by tangible improvements in your energy levels and physical strength - can transform your thirst for alcohol into a distant memory, replaced entirely by an unquenchable curiosity about the world and your own potential within it.

Fitness also empowers you to turn your demons into a source of strength. You can literally lift yourself out of alcohol cravings, depression, and anxiety. The gym starts out as purgatory, but over time it becomes a high temple. When you transform yourself on a molecular level, feelings of deprivation evaporate.

There was a time in my life when I surrendered to the reality of my alcohol addiction. This is the only time I've ever surrendered, and I did not take that word to mean that my life would be just okay. Even if I lived alone on a desert island, I would rather die than feel as if I were a mediocre version of whatever I could be on that island.

Mediocre goals are impotent. When we aim for the bare minimum in life, we often find ourselves uninspired to do anything at all. Those of us who beat addiction tend to have an all-or-nothing mentality. If we want to be okay, we should try to grow ourselves well beyond the ashes of our past addictions.

Have you ever noticed that minor things bother you more on your days off? You stay home to relax, but you stub your toe and feel restless and can't figure out what to eat for lunch. Your perception of life's difficulty is subjective. The ultimate irony is that sitting in a chair and "recovering" forever is actually harder than putting addiction in the past, taking on new challenges, and striving to be totally fulfilled.

Happiness is not a destination. It is a balanced state of being in which your body, mind, and life's purpose align for the benefit of others as well as yourself. It is not static, but rather a state of evolving growth. It is progress.

Have you ever had a moment in which you just knew that you were born to do something? We're happiest when we push ourselves slightly beyond the boundaries of our abilities; when we pursue, and therefore grow. People with the highest overall levels of happiness are those who do not shy away from risk, challenge, and adversity.

I'm not saying that you have to accumulate worldly things. Maybe your calling is to get out of your own head and spend more time with your family. Maybe it involves escaping into the jungle and pursuing divine knowledge in a cave. Spark your internal fire and go wherever it leads you.

Three Tips for Success

After I left the corporate world, I began training people in the gym as a way to make some money until I found a new mission. I've observed that people who who achieve their goals both inside and outside of the gym follow three rules in everything they do:

- **Don't self-sabotage**: Overanalyzing, second-guessing, and minimizing the importance of today are the weapons of your false subconscious assumptions. Self-sabotage is the logical consequence of feeling undeserving of happiness on a subconscious level.

- **Bounce back from small failures**: The ability to perceive failure as valuable feedback is far more potent than raw willpower. This book would not exist if I hadn't failed to quit drinking literally hundreds of times.

- **Never give up**: If you fail to get results, keep learning and tweaking your strategies and goals. Once you make a habit of finding opportunities for growth amidst chaos and negativity, you will naturally transform into a stress-resistant optimist.

I've also found that it's best to break down big goals into tiny pieces. My first workouts after detoxing consisted of 10 minutes of light cardio and three sets each on two machines. Over time, I built myself up from there. The most pathetic workout in the world is a heroic feat when you haven't yet made exercise a habit. Remind yourself that no matter how bad you feel before your workout, you'll always feel better afterward.

The same rule holds true outside of the gym. You'll never go to bed regretting that you gave something your all.

CHAPTER 10

CHOOSE YOUR TRIBE

"Resolve to throw off the influences of any unfortunate
environment, and to build your own life to order."
-Napoleon Hill

I have already mentioned the rise of the self-improvement ethos, and I want to share a hunch that I have. I suspect that more people are now quitting drinking with the help of online communities than with physical support groups. Which is to say, of those 90% of people who try and fail to sustain meetings, a large percentage are changing their habits and attitudes with the help of interpersonal connections (reciprocated or not) forged through their computers and smartphones.

I say this because I'm one of these people. Of the thousands of discussion threads, blogs, podcasts, and YouTube channels, I only check a few of them, and I do not always agree with the content. What strikes me as strange is that many of these online communities have nothing at all to do with alcohol addiction; yet at the same time, I can say definitively that I've taken more out of Joe Rogan's podcast, Rhonda Patrick's YouTube videos, and haphazard discussions on Reddit than I ever have out of any traditional recovery support group that limits itself to discussing alcohol addiction.

We're living in a cultural renaissance of sorts, in which the established ways of doing things - like trusting powerful corporations to provide us with our news, or in our case, assuming there is only one way to quit drinking - are being overturned by ordinary people with unprecedented power to spread their messages. I mentioned the rise of self-improvement communities on the web, which tend to agree about some broad principles and yet differ sharply with regard to specific issues.

Different tribes cater to different groups; there is something for everyone. The common person, who approaches the web for specific answers to a specific problem, ends up unintentionally joining one or more tribes that unify self-improvement with tribal belonging, intellectual enlightenment, sensory bliss, and - most crucially - a renewed sense of curiosity about our rapidly changing world. This is a powerful weapon against addiction that deserves to be discussed.

Unless you don't have a modem, I'm not informing you of the existence of online tribes. I'm mentioning something you already know and affirming its power to help you change your life. Human beings are tribal animals, and if we do not already, we will soon live in a world in which everyone has multiple tribal identities - the primary one established within our immediate family and/or friends, and the others molded by our trusted online sources of information, advice, and entertainment. If I'm correct in assuming that you're inclined to join at least a few different tribes, most of which have nothing to do with addiction, then this is a vindication of a central premise of this book: that your life is not defined by your past addiction.

The line between dominating alcohol and living a fulfilling life, enriched by a sense of mission and strong relationships, is fine and blurry. I know that replenishing my physiology, making exercise a habit, and reprogramming my mind were necessary to get beyond the phase of craving alcohol - a phase that often lasts forever for people who never discover these methods on their own. I know that I never would have appreciated anything if I had accepted false ideas about alcohol's inherent value or refused to get off my couch and force my brain to rewire through weightlifting.

Recovery is a phase; it does not need to be a permanent state of existence. You can make it a permanent state if you convince yourself that it is. But being a nondrinker with a past addiction is not like being in remission from cancer. If you were placed on a desert island and had to survive like Robinson Crusoe, you would not wake up obsessing about your "disease." As you fished, hunted, dealt with wildlife and built yourself shelters, you would see that the view of alcohol addiction as a lifelong curse is really just a social construction based on mass preference for a particular toxin. Since this preference is assumed to be universal, you are assumed to have a devastating and life-depriving disease. This is very silly.

You might be interested to know that Robinson Crusoe is based on a real 18th century Scotsman, named Alexander Selkirk - who lived alone on a Pacific island, hunting and taming cats and goats, and who discovered that he had completely lost his taste for alcohol when he returned to Britain.

I'm not saying that the solution to addiction is to live alone on a desert island. I'm making the point that your decisions about whom you allow to influence your thoughts - your mental frames - are yours alone. These decisions will have a lasting impact on your quality of life. Give yourself time to consciously choose your inner circle, consisting of people you associate with on a daily basis, as well as the more distant tribes that you choose to join.

I was extremely lucky to discover that my family and the great friends I had made years ago were willing to support my efforts to change my life. If I had heeded the common advice to ditch all the people you used to get drinks with and build a new tribe of "sober friends," I'm certain that I would have become guilty, miserable, and surrounded by chronic relapsers. Dispose of toxic friendships, but understand that not everyone who still drinks is your enemy.

Nearly all of my best friends are social drinkers. A few of them have privately told me that they suspect our heavy drinking culture is a pervasive trap. Even though they are not addicted to alcohol, they have cut down on drinking tremendously, in part because I've unintentionally demonstrated to them that drinking is not a necessary ingredient in a fulfilling life.

What should you do if you realize that the people you thought were your friends were really just drinking buddies? A few people I used to think were amazingly fun turned out to be quite bland when separated from alcohol and other drugs. This isn't tragic, it's just part of transcending addiction. If this problem plagues your entire inner circle, then it's time to find new friends.

Before I quit drinking, I painfully ended a relationship with a girl I had been dating for two years. I ended it because when I told her of my intentions to quit drinking, she responded: "I can't date someone who doesn't drink." Her inability to empathize with me was not necessarily her fault - we live in a society obsessed with drinking, and I was not a picture of contrarian strength when I asked for support - but it hurt for a long time. Having witnessed my downward spiral, she concluded that I could redeem myself if I proved that I could drink moderately. I knew that I could not be a member of a tribe, much less a romantic partnership, that made alcohol a priority.

I met many new and interesting people after I beat addiction. I avoided sober fanatics who see the world through the lens of "sobriety" - or worse, deprivation. My support came mainly from people who had always been there for me, and from new friendships that had nothing to do with either alcohol or abstinence. In my experience, the easiest way to make new friends in a culture dominated by drinking is to ask an acquaintance you respect to be your workout buddy. Fitness is universally valued and the gym is one of the few places where people don't have the option of relying on alcohol to establish bonds. Moreover, working out releases oxytocin and endorphins, which will naturally deepen your bond with your lifting (or running, or yoga, or boxing) buddy.

When you transform yourself from a depressed alcohol-dependent into a fit nondrinker, your personal life will improve drastically. After I reached a certain level of confidence, I went on many coffee dates just to see what was out there. I was surprised to discover that most women didn't just not care that I didn't drink; the vast majority of them admired me for it. One of them told me that I'd changed her assumptions about drinking - not because I said anything about drinking, but because we had so much fun without it. We had gone out to dinner several times and she drank heavily the first two times. By our third date, she decided not to drink at all, and got emotional when she told me that was now having more fun than when she drank.

In our culture, developing the self-confidence to have fun without "needing" to drink to calm your nerves is a significant achievement. People who agree to coffee dates are generally more confident and stable than those who insist on drinking.

After dozens of coffee dates, I'd met only three (!) people who felt uncomfortable with the fact that I didn't drink. Two out of those three had all of the silent telltale signs of alcohol addiction. The last one was a party girl with a dependent personality type; she subjected all things and people to a popularity contest based on external groupthink. If you avoid this type of person, which is easily identifiable among both males and females, you'll have no trouble having fun with people without drinking.

If you join a tribe - whether in person or online - that really appeals to you, see if there are other people in your area who share your enthusiasm. Common interests are the basis for solid friendships and relationships. In my case, the blogs and podcasts I follow are continual topics of discussion with my closest friends. We tend to be idea-centered, always exploring new possibilities and novel ways of viewing the world. No topic of discussion is off-limits or unworthy. Not everyone shares this mode of perception. Find people who see the world through a lens that you understand and appreciate.

The following chapter condenses this book into highly actionable steps. While I do not want to spend the rest of my life pondering alcohol addiction, I do want to help many people discover and experience the same breakthroughs that helped me beat addiction.

Feel free to check out my website, Fit Recovery (Fit-Recovery.com) for additional information and updates on my activities.

It's time to get MOVING. It's time to get HIGH ON LIFE. And it's time to set yourself up to become more FULFILLED than you ever thought possible.

CHAPTER 11

THE 30 DAY PROGRAM

"I've watched you. You're about to do something. You've made
yourself very strong."
-Athelstan, speaking to Ragnar, *Vikings*

Knowledge is just the beginning of your transformation.

Below is the fast track for dominating alcohol addiction forever.

Overthinking things never got you anywhere.

What you need now is decisive action.

THE 30 DAY PROGRAM FOR DOMINATING ALCOHOL

(I suggest adding your own notes in a journal for each step.)

1. Taper off of alcohol, or withdraw with the help of medications
from your doctor, or under medical supervision if you have serious
withdrawal (as I did).

For more information on tapering methods and natural alcohol withdrawal remedies, subscribe to my email list at Fit-Recovery.com.

Do not proceed to Step 2 until you have quit drinking alcohol.

Then, follow Steps 2-12 for 30 DAYS. Since I am not a doctor and cannot give medical advice, please consult your doctor before taking any supplements or changing your lifestyle in any way.

2. Take the following basic supplements at recommended dosages (and times of day) for 30 days:

    _____ **High Quality Multivitamin**
    _____ **B Vitamin Complex**
    _____ **Vitamin C**
    _____ **Vitamin D3**
    _____ **Magnesium Citrate**
    _____ **Omega-3 Fish Oil (and/or GLA)**
    _____ **L-Glutamine**
    _____ **DL-Phenylalanine**
    _____ **L-Tyrosine**
    _____ **L-Tryptophan or 5HTP***

*Do not take L-Tryptophan or 5HTP if you take an SSRI antidepressant.

(On Day 1, take DL-Phenylalanine in the morning, L-Tyrosine in the afternoon, and L-Tryptophan/5HTP before bed. See how you feel after taking each. If one of these does not agree with your system, return it to the manufacturer.)

To see my current brand recommendations for the basic supplements outlined above, and more: Go to Fit-Recovery.com/DrinkingSucks and use DrinkingSucks as the password.

3. Make a list of substitutes for unhealthy foods and beverages (that you regularly consume) and stick to these substitutes.

4. Do the PASS routine every morning upon waking up. Also try it before a stressful situation.

5. Find a workout buddy with whom to do some form of cardio or weightlifting at least three times per week.

6. Disrupt anxiety by fixing your posture, rolling your shoulders back and straightening your spine. Take deep breaths through your nose and hold them for a second before exhaling through your mouth.

7. Take one 15-30 minute meditation break every day. Pick a mantra that you can associate with letting go of self-criticism, worry, and fear.

8. Keep a running list of new reframes for alcohol whenever you think of them. Cross out rationalizations for drinking and underline your reframes next to them.

9. Fully develop one anchor, of your choice, that makes you feel positive, confident, or even euphoric on command.

10. Write down a reasonable 30-day goal that has nothing to do with drinking or "sobriety." Set aside time every day to work on your goal.

11. Read every night before bed. During the day, find blogs, podcasts, audiobooks, etc. that indulge your curiosities.

12. Sunday is your day of rest from all exercise (including PASS routine) and your day for one big cheat meal. Pig out. Don't ruin it by eating too much beforehand!

At the end of 30 days, regardless of your starting point, you will move onto a higher plane of consciousness.

If you feel "off" after ending the supplement regime, you can use trial and error to determine which supplements you may benefit from continuing. Once your system is balanced, you can stop taking the supplements. Keep your remaining supplements in case you ever need them again.

As you rebuild your brain, body and mind, you will dissolve the chains of alcohol addiction forever. You will look better. You will feel happy. Your newfound strength will compound with time.

You can begin your 30 Day Plan now. In the remaining chapters of this book, I will strive to provide you with additional information and inspiration that will enhance your journey.

CHAPTER 12

HERBS THAT ACTUALLY WORK

"Things in nature like basil and coriander can't be patented so there
isn't a lot of money thrown at them."
-Mark Schatzker, *The Dorito Effect*

The most absurd thought that entered my mind when I quit drinking
was this: "Whelp, now I'm not allowed to relax anymore."

Fast forward a few years, and I'm relaxing every night with a clear
mind. My ridiculous thought was merely a symptom of protracted
alcohol withdrawal. I could have avoided it if I'd repaired my brain
sooner.

Happy people who have beaten addiction tend to have rituals that
they turn to regularly to calm their minds. I know an older guy who
hasn't had a drink in 30 years, and every day since then he's used a
very specific form of Buddhist meditation. After exercise, my
favorite ritual involves turning on a couple of himalayan salt lamps
and making a nightly pitcher of very potent chamomile tea.

Chamomile has been used for centuries to ease anxiety, depression
and insomnia. Research is slowly figuring out what our ancestors
knew long ago. Studies that have been done on herbs like chamomile,
passionflower, and lemon balm have found that they are incredibly
effective alternatives to anti-anxiety drugs.

Chamomile contains dozens of natural compounds that gently and synergistically mimic the effects of anti-anxiety pills. Interestingly, instead of building a tolerance to herbs like chamomile, we tend to respond more favorably to them as time goes on. Habits are not the same thing as chemical addictions: unlike alcohol and drugs, chamomile does not create withdrawal that only chamomile can resolve. The reason people don't drink chamomile tea more often is because one teabag has such a mild effect that it's almost unnoticeable.

You'll really feel the calming effect if you use six tea bags. Since I don't want to run to the bathroom all night, I'll let the bags steep for 10 minutes in a pitcher with just enough water for one strong cup. I'll throw in a few different types of tea bags for extra aroma, along with half a teaspoon of organic honey. This ritual helps me to relax and read a book until my eyes get tired and sleep comes easily.

Since there's no reason to waste 6 tea bags, I'll fill the pitcher again with cold filtered water and keep it in the fridge. It makes for a relaxing alternative to coffee the following afternoon.

I've had this nighttime ritual for over two years, and a funny thing happened recently when I was watching a show. The main character filled a tin cup with some indiscriminate liquid from a large pitcher. I caught myself assuming for a second that he was about to drink some strong chamomile tea, as I was doing while watching him. While this is funny and nonsensical, it's also proof that my brain associates my obscure ritual, rather than alcohol, with relaxation and pleasure.

I've sipped on strong chamomile tea at holiday get-togethers while everyone else is drinking spiked egg nog and wine. It's nice to have your own relaxing drink. I savor the aroma and assess the color when I pour it out of the pitcher and into my mug. At summer barbecues, I'll add some mango tea bags and pour it over ice in a huge wine glass. People who don't know me assume that I'm drinking something, and people who do know me think, "Well, he's got his own beverage, and he's clearly having fun." That's damn right - and there's evidence that my elixir improves my skin, helps my mental functioning, and prevents cancer.

The same can't be said about alcohol, which has been classified as a carcinogen since 1988 and more recently been linked to seven types of cancers. Quitting alcohol gives you an opportunity to sample the wide range of delicious beverages - from herbal teas to fresh juices and exotic coffees - that give you a noticeable mood boost and even performance enhancement without threatening your vitality.

In my mid-twenties, my nightly ritual involved opening a bottle of hard liquor and drinking it straight out of a tall glass while mindlessly watching TV and wondering whether I should order a pizza. My life has improved since then, and now you know all of the steps I took to get here. Herbs alone won't cure addiction, but they can further balance your physiology and fill ritualistic voids when you quit drinking.

More Herbs for Mood Support & Body Repair

Chamomile is the only herb I consume every day. However, many others can provide mood support while recovering from addiction. I've tried so many herbs that I've considered writing a book about them. The vast majority of them did absolutely nothing, but a few stood out as exceptional.

Do not take any herbs or supplements without consulting first with your doctor.

- **CBD Oil** - This is the newest and most exciting addition to my herbal collection. CBD has been shown in recent studies to reduce systemic inflammation and possibly protect against alcohol cravings and relapse. The brand I use is extracted from industrial hemp (not marijuana) and can be found on my website, Fit-Recovery.com.

- **Mucuna Pruriens** - I took this herb several times per week in the first year I quit drinking, and it helped erase mental fog, increase motivation, and improve sleep. This herb contains the building blocks of dopamine and noticeably shifted my brain out of post-acute withdrawal syndrome.

- **Passionflower** - One dropper of the glycerin extract (non-alcoholic) helps me get to sleep at night.

- **Lemon Balm** - Nature's Way capsules, which sell for around $5 per bottle, help me to relax and drift off to sleep effortlessly.

- **Ashwagandha** - I still occasionally take this amazing adaptogenic herb for mood support - it has the unique ability to enhance relaxation AND focus.

- **Rhodiola Rosea** - I've found noticeable relief from fatigue from this herb, which helps restore adrenal health.

- **Bacopa Monnieri** - I've experienced a sharper mind after taking this herb for a few weeks.

Finally, I've had great results combining **Fenugreek**, **Maca Root**, and **D-Asapartic Acid** (an amino acid, not an herb) for sustaining energy levels and feeling like a man again after beating addiction.

If you drank enough to strain your liver, I recommend taking **Milk Thistle** for a few months. This herb will not directly affect your mood but it has been scientifically proven to help support liver function, even in people with cirrhosis and other forms of chemical poisoning. A healthy liver is necessary for a sense of well-being.

Years ago, I tried and failed to quit drinking alcohol while taking **Kudzu Root**. However, I did notice a temporary decline in my drinking while taking this herb. If can quit drinking on your own without major withdrawal, give this herb a try.

I know people who swear by **Holy Basil** for shutting off racing thoughts and falling asleep quickly. This herb had no effect on me, but since I seem to be the exception, it's worth mentioning.

The bottom line is that there ARE natural herbs, which humans have used for centuries or more, that are gentler, cheaper, and often more effective than synthetic chemicals produced by Big Pharma. While they are generally very safe, everyone's physiology is different, and so trial and error is the best approach.

CHAPTER 13

ON GOING TEETOTAL

"I personally believe that the majority of people who have down moments in their lives, they can actually trace it back, quite often, to alcohol."
-Sir Richard Branson, on *The Tim Ferris Show*

Teetotal is a funny adjective. I like it more than the word *sober*. If you're teetotal, you're unique and you might confuse people who can't imagine plodding through life without alcohol. That's their problem; you have the right to be your own person.

Unlike many sober people, who see alcohol as a mischievous devil permanently perched on their shoulder, I see alcohol as a moot substance. It's simply a waste of my time and vital energy. I drank too much for a decade before quitting about three years ago.

Not only did I refuse to sacrifice my social life, I've had more fun these past four years as a teetotaler than I ever did as a drinker.

If you want to know what it takes to navigate modern society without drinking AND without sacrificing your fun, independence, and dignity, then read on.

I'm going to use some personal anecdotes to help me explain my strategies for going teetotal at dinners, parties, and weddings.

Dinners & Dates

I used to see dates, banquets and special occasions as excuses for getting hammered. This is a self-limiting mentality that many "social" binge-drinkers subscribe to. Going teetotal and sticking with your decision is much more fun than living in an alcoholic haze.

However, I did suffer from major alcohol cravings when I quit drinking. I remember not knowing whether it was possible for me to have fun without drinking.

Over time, I realized that the desire to drink, aside from the physical compulsion of alcoholics, is largely a social construct. We are not hardwired to want to drink, but we are hardwired to want to enjoy the company of other people. My past belief that it was impossible to enjoy dates and dinners without alcohol was a myth, and I was the only one who could refute it for myself.

When you're out with a small to medium sized group of people, the fun you have while teetotaling will depend on three things:

• Your energy level
• Your sociability level
• The quality of the people you're out with

The bad news is that it's hard to have fun with a rude date or a group of boring people. This is not really bad news. Life is too short to waste your time hanging out with subpar people.

I used to work with number crunchers who happened to be extremely bland. Their idea of a good time was to go out to go to a club and finish a few bottles of vodka while barely talking to each other. I left my job and never had to deal with them again. It was worth being poor for awhile to get away from these psychopaths and make awesome new friends.

People say that alcohol makes other people more interesting. In reality, it makes drinkers self-satisfied and easily entertained by boring things. This is not an ideal state of mind for special occasions, which are best spent with people whom you find genuinely uplifting and interesting. The only total solution is to take total control of your life so that you don't have to spend your leisure time with people who aren't worth your time.

The good news is that with practice, you can improve your own energy levels and sociability to almost make up for being out with a bland group of people. I work out before going on dates so that my endorphins are flowing by the time I arrive. I've seen wit, charm, and humor on the part of one individual transform a dead dinner into raucous cascades of laughter.

Reading self-improvement blogs and books can help you devise strategies to increase your energy and sociability. Learning NLP can also be very useful for controlling your emotions and influencing other people.

Also, some people who seem boring at first are simply reluctant to open up. Try to see this as a challenge you can solve rather than an intractable problem. Shortly after I quit drinking, I spent some time with a great girl who was very shy. She used alcohol to loosen up for the first few dates. After she became comfortable around me, she told me that she thought it was refreshing that I don't drink. She then stopped drinking around me – not for my sake, but for her own. We went on bike rides, walks in the park, and went to small parties in which all of our friends knew that I didn't drink.

I have a good friend who entertains clients at boozy dinners as part of his managerial duties. He's recently quit drinking, which is a difficult feat in such a position. As he gets further away from alcohol, I think he'll begin to see that people silently respect him for teetotaling. If you're in a similar position, there are a few other strategies that can help:

• Remember that most people who ask you why you're not drinking are genuinely curious, rather than determined to change your lifestyle.

- If you're great at what you do, you feel great, and you look great – you're well dressed and you clearly respect your body – then no one can make fun of you without looking like a toxic loser.

- To drunks who are offended by your teetotaling, say that you have a rare condition – just one drink can give you a migraine, make you break out in hives, or send you to the bathroom.

For the past several years, I've been upfront about my teetotaling before going on dates. Out of dozens of coffee dates and even bar dates, only 4 girls have refused to meet me because I don't drink. Somehow, girls who have turned out to be the heaviest drinkers have admired my teetotaling the most: "I wish I could do it / I don't know how you do it!" is a very common response when I tell them I don't drink.

With that said, I've been surprised at how many people actually prefer not to drink on dates. It seems like every other girl out there has an alcoholic ex-boyfriend who she's relieved to be rid of.

I don't make any excuses for why I don't drink. I simply say that I used to drink too much, so I quit, and now my life is much more enjoyable. I make clear that this was my personal decision and I don't judge anyone who drinks. 99% of people will respect you if you've given up alcohol because you once had a problem, as long as you don't preach about it.

Parties & Weddings

The strategies I discussed above also work for going teetotal at larger parties and weddings. There are a few key differences from smaller gatherings and intimate dates, in my experience:

- If you're genuinely close to whoever is throwing the big party or wedding, it will be a blast because you have something to celebrate with people you actually care about.

- If you're a guest or you simply don't click with the people present, there's nothing wrong with simply making an appearance and leaving early.

- All of your friends lining up for tequila shots at the wedding party bar can be frustrating or a funny spectacle, depending on how you choose to frame it.

- Drunk conversations between strangers that happen after midnight are rarely worth sticking around for; you're not missing out by going home and sleeping.

- If you're having fun but getting tired, most bars serve coffee – I met up with some great friends last NYE and was able to stay conversational until 2 AM this way.

I had a hard time with sudden alcohol cravings for months after I gave up alcohol. It wasn't that I needed alcohol, it was that my body wanted sugar, didn't have enough magnesium to feel relaxed, didn't get enough sunlight (vitamin D), and my brain didn't produce enough serotonin and dopamine. At a wedding only a few months after I quit drinking, it was tough for me to sit there feeling mildly subpar while my friends laughed over shots. This moment soon passed though, and I had a great time at the rest of the wedding because I was with great people.

My alcohol cravings went away because I tackled my nutrition proactively. I also ramped up my workouts until my physique became a point of pride. Eventually, my fitness level morphed into an unintended conversation piece when I met up with old friends. Not only do I not feel cravings anymore, but I don't want to contaminate my hard won progress.

It might sound arrogant, but these days I often suspect that people who drink around me are trying to get on my level of well-being. I don't judge them or pity them; they have the right to do whatever makes them feel good. I used to drink more than all of them and I ruined my body for years. My priority is to enjoy being fit and feeling great. If other people want to drink, that's their business, but I've been there and done that. On to new things!

My Preferred Alternatives To Alcohol

I'm not one to preach against mind-alteration. I simply see alcohol as a subpar means to this end. It's in the same mental bucket as developing a new cigarette habit or doing whippets every night after work.

Instead of doing silly things, I use meditation, breathing techniques and exercise to alter my state of mind almost every day. I've also used a number of supplements, herbs and drugs that are much safer than alcohol.

I absolutely don't recommend that you use all of my recommendations recklessly, but they are worth knowing about in case they can occasionally enhance your quality of life. I have mixed views on prescription drugs, which I think are generally overused but useful in specific circumstances.

Below is a list of substances that are both potentially useful and safer than alcohol. I'm not a doctor, and none of this is medical advice. Consult with a medical professional before trying anything new.

- **Yerba Mate** – This tea from South America creates a mild yet uplifting natural high. I will often consume it before dates, because it has the unique ability to relax my mind and energize my body. It is the perfect substitute for coffee and does not cause any jitters. If you're trying to cut down your coffee consumption, you'll avoid withdrawal and feel better if you start switching to yerba mate.

- **Kava** – This ground root from the Pacific islands contains kavalactones, which induce relaxation and even euphoria. There are bars in the U.S. that serve kava instead of alcohol. Every time I've been to Tropikava in Chicago, I've had stimulating conversations with friends while sipping delicious, kava-infused concoctions made with almond milk, cinnamon, and nutmeg. My favorite kava strains make me feel relaxed and euphoric.

- **Kratom** – This herb is a godsend for people with chronic pain and post-acute withdrawal syndrome. As with phenibut, daily use can cause addiction. It causes a sense of heightened well-being, with variations depending on the strain. Along with phenibut, kratom is a good option for teetotalers who want to attend a once in a lifetime concert or a party. I never use kratom for multiple days in a row, because it can lead to coffee-like dependence over time. (Note: Kratom is not legal everywhere. Check its legal status in your place of residence before opting for this plant!)

- **Marijuana** – I'm not a pot head and I don't recommend that you become one either, but let's be honest: as a drug, weed is much safer than alcohol. It kills zero people each year while alcohol kills 88,000. This fact alone should help you see how irrational the groupthink surrounding alcohol really is. Millions of people with severe social anxiety and medical conditions are helped by this plant. As with kratom, marijuana is not legal everywhere.

- **Phenibut** – This nootropic supplement was developed to treat anxiety in Soviet astronauts. I've used it before long airplane flights with great results. It does not create any sort of high in low doses, but it does create a "smooth sailing" feeling. It takes several hours to kick in and can be used occasionally to prevent social anxiety. I use it before taking long airplane flights. Take care, because daily use can lead to dependence.

- **Propranolol** – This is a prescription drug that combats severe situational anxiety without providing any euphoria. A beta-blocker, it simply prevents adrenaline from building up in your bloodstream and makes it impossible for you to have a panic attack. Because it does not cause any sort of high, it is non-addictive. Propranolol can be effective for people who are in early recovery from alcoholism and want to prevent panic attacks in nerve-wracking situations without resorting to benzodiazepines. In the months after I quit drinking alcohol, propranolol helped me to maintain my composure during several stressful events. I rarely use it anymore.

Going teetotal is far from the end of the world. You can navigate the social dilemmas posed by not drinking in a culture obsessed with alcohol. Most importantly, you may just discover some new ways to enhance your personality and your health.

Your most memorable experiences will have very little to do with the amount of alcohol present. One thing I've learned since I quit drinking is that great times stand out more in my memory. On many of these occasions, other people were drinking and I was not.

Moreover, my own teetotaling never stands out as my defining memory of these events. I remember great conversations, friendly faces, positive vibes, and the ambiance or scenery of whatever the venues were. I'm glad that I didn't avoid my long-time friends just because I'd quit drinking. I naturally fell out of touch with the few friends I had who were simply alcoholic drinking buddies.

I also remind myself that alcohol is a poisonous, temporary route to mind-alteration. A great workout creates endorphins for hours. Eating healthy food improves your energy levels. If you're anxious, tired, or depressed, look into nutritional supplements that can repair your physiology.

If you still can't seem to feel your best without alcohol, don't give up!

I have medicine cabinets filled with supplements as a kind of insurance policy, just in case I need them at a later date. Over the past four years, I've created my own apothecary-style bar with everything from ginseng and obscure adaptogen teas to CBD oil and various strains of kava and kratom.

Above all else, respect your brain. Learn your limitations and stop dabbling in things that don't mix well with your physiology. Find what works for you. But don't ever let alcohol hold a toxic monopoly on your definition of fun.

CHAPTER 14

MATT'S STORY

(This chapter was first published as an article on Fit-Recovery.com on September 9th, 2017.)

When Matt reached out to me, I realized that he was earnestly searching for answers. He saw that something was missing in mainstream recovery for the independent and promising person who suffers from a false need for alcohol.

To his credit, Matt had already quit drinking when we began talking. His next step was to overcome post-acute withdrawal syndrome (PAWS) so that he could confidently stay away from alcohol, rewire his brain, and live the best life that he could dream of.

From the first time we talked, I could tell that Matt had something that many people lack – something that I like to call internal fire. He was 100% committed to seeking and finding the answers that he needed to put an end to the vicious cycle of drinking, abstinence, anxiety, depression, and relapse.

There is no "one size fits all" recovery model that works, but Matt is living proof that anyone can prevail over alcohol addiction and post-acute withdrawal syndrome (PAWS) with a blend of biochemical repair and core convictions tailored to their unique needs.

Here is Matt's story, told in his own words.

A Familiar Routine

I grew up in a home of moderate daily drinkers, where it was normal to come home from a hard day at work and crack a few cold ones.

At around the age of seventeen, I developed a taste for alcohol after a bad relationship breakup. I would compensate my father every week for whatever amount of beer I desired.

But my habit didn't develop into a dangerous one overnight. I wasn't drinking and driving, I would never consume more than 3-4 drinks at a time (except on special occasions), and I could still have fun without alcohol.

The First Red Flag

From the ages of 18 to 21, there wasn't a day when I didn't have at least a few drinks.

Slowly it worsened, and things reached a tipping point by the time I hit 21.

Newly emancipated from the dreaded schoolmaster, I entered adulthood and found myself suffering from extreme anxiety and a toxic relationship that made my insides scream for relief. Alcohol was the answer, or so I thought. Parties and hangovers became a normal routine, until one day it all came to a head.

I had a full-blown panic attack right in the middle of a church service.

My life became a nightmare. For months, I suffered from confusion, panic, depression, and a laundry list of negative emotions. My behavior deteriorated rapidly. Had alcohol caused my panic, depressed nature, and ever-increasing bad decisions?

After the panic attack, I quit booze cold turkey, which is a bad idea for anyone who has been drinking every day for years. I didn't know much about recovery, and I suspected that AA was for those special people who'd drink hard liquor every day, all day, right? For the first couple of weeks in my sobriety I went through mild DT's.

The lows were horrendous and literally nothing made me happy.

Everything under the sun was almost unbearable, and a black cloud consumed everything. But as I progressed, my symptoms regressed a little. I found myself with two months of liberation under my belt.

Missing Out On The Fun

I was proud, but my mind was still screaming, "lets have a drink— you can handle it—you're missing out on all the fun!"

And so I drank again.

This quitting and starting over would occur on and off for the next 4-5 years.

My abuse worsened, and I went from drinking 2-3 drinks a night to at least 6, along with all weekend party bingers. Not to mention, I'd drive home 30 miles drunk nearly every day from work.

It is truly a miracle that I hadn't been caught, killed, or worse, killed someone else.

Many people can precisely tell of their rock bottom event. I can't, because I feel as if all those years were my "rock-bottom." My relationships, job, outlook, motivation, and future were all tremendously affected by my drinking. Nothing made me as happy as alcohol and everything I did while intoxicated felt so magical.

I knew this was a heap of lies. I felt like I'd had enough, and I was sick and tired of being sick and tired!

Although I said that every time I tried quitting drinking, I never changed anything.

My friends stayed the same, I never pursued recovery, my diet sucked, and I never exercised.

Doing Battle With PAWS

I decided to quit once again on February 20, 2017.

What I couldn't understand was how badly I felt after I quit drinking. It had happened before. Anywhere between 1-4 weeks after quitting, anxiety and depression would hit me like a ton of bricks. It's difficult to describe.

It felt as if someone had turned off a switch and made everything very, very hard.

I could only focus on trying to survive, day by day.

This time, through providence, God placed some great people in my life. I threw off my old "friends" and formed new, empowering relationships with people who held me accountable. I joined a recovery group and attended religiously.

And luckily, this go-around I stumbled upon a website called Fit-Recovery.com, run by a guy named Chris Scott.

I reached out and got a quick response that calmed me down a bit. Being a former alcoholic himself, he could relate and his website was full of valuable recovery information. I signed up for a coaching session and we began communicating regularly.

Chris explained that booze had put a monopoly on my brain chemicals for years and it would take time, proper nutrition and exercise to get myself re-balanced.

At first I was doubtful, but if you do the research, there is a treasure-trove of credible scientific information that backs up these claims. Alcohol depletes essential vitamins and minerals, alters brain chemistry, and directly affects levels of dopamine, serotonin, and endorphins.

I learned that what I was experiencing was called PAWS (post-acute withdrawal syndrome), which can last anywhere from months to years after quitting drinking.

PAWS happens because brain chemicals do not rebalance overnight from years of daily drinking. This results often in chronic anxiety, depression, restlessness, and insomnia. If you're not proactive, your brain might never fully heal.

Finding A Recovery That Fits

Everyone's recovery process is different, and I don't claim to have the answer. But I can testify that exercise, diet, and supplementation did help my recovery process, and they especially helped me get over PAWS.

Exercise is now a regular part of my routine. It's been scientifically proven that exercise rewires the brain and can be as effective as anti-depressants. Now, a hard run or lift will automatically boost my mood significantly.

Once I started exercising regularly and taking the supplements that I needed, I found that I had a powerhouse of tools to ignite my recovery.

Alcohol seriously depletes vitamins A, B's, C, D, and magnesium. Along with some minor diet changes (reducing sugar) and amino acids that Chris recommended, these were the supplements that helped me the most. My body had suffered from heavy drinking for years, and restoring all of these nutrients was essential for my physical and mental health.

For me, sobriety is a lifestyle that does not have to be dreadful.

On the contrary, I can attest that life without booze is much more meaningful once you balance your brain. Brain neuroplasticity is a somewhat recent scientific discovery. Once I learned about neuroplasticity, I realized that I could undo the damage done to my brain by alcohol and bad decisions.

Surrounding myself with honest, good-hearted folk and digging into my faith were another couple keys to my recovery. I got involved in a church program called Celebrate Recovery, which I recommend to everyone. For me, what started out as alcohol recovery morphed into a hard examination of every aspect of my personal life.

In just a few months, I've seen some dramatic spiritual changes and created some true, solid friendships.

Although I do not condemn Alcoholics Anonymous, I simply could not attend their meetings. AA meetings felt depressing and hopeless to me. My 12-step program works for me, in a place where I'm surrounded by positive, Godly people that believe in actual change, without a label.

The View From 6 Months

I don't have to categorize myself as hopeless or helpless, because I'm not.

I do not have to live with the limiting belief that alcohol owns me, because it doesn't.

I am a marvelous human being who was created by God to heal myself and others, not regress into negativity, disempowering beliefs or hopelessness.

So, what's six months of sobriety like after 8 years of alcohol-induced misery?

Inexplicably amazing! For years I could never enjoy much of anything.

Now, the simple things are meaningful: sunsets, reading, social interactions, and even work.

For once, I have a positive outlook on life and am genuinely excited!

My business has improved and I've started school. I'm in a passionate, loving, and healthy relationship. And I have more time, money, and consciousness.

Yes, life has gotten much, much better and it's only been six months.

I cannot wait to see what the rest of my life will look like.

CHAPTER 15

TANA'S STORY

(This chapter was first published as an article on Fit-Recovery.com on August 20th, 2018.)

Like many people, Tana felt somewhat reluctant to share her story. I'm extremely proud of her for allowing other people to benefit from her perspective.

I will let Tana speak for herself, but I will say that her hard-won victory is a reminder that alcohol recovery is often nonlinear.

We can hit horrible lows, climb out slowly, reach new highs, and then fall all the way back to square one before discovering the missing links in our recovery and FINALLY breaking the chains of alcohol addiction.

Tana reminds us that when you change your biochemistry, you can change your life.

Her story is also a testament to the fact that nothing great is ever accomplished without tremendous internal resolve.

Traumatic Beginnings

My family moved again. I had been to countless schools at this point. This time, my family moved me to a new school in a small town a few months into my first year in high school.

Being a freshman in high school was scary enough. Now I was the new girl after everyone had already gotten acquainted. I had to get adjusted to high school and then get readjusted to a new school with new students. I was thirteen years old.

It was hard for me to decipher who would be *my people*. I had grown up always wanting to do the right thing. I didn't care that I didn't fit in because I would rather not do the things the "cool kids" were doing and just do me and follow my faith.

But, here it was different. I was tired of moving and having to make new friends. As you get older, kids seem to get more malevolent, and I was tired of being picked on for my "good girl" persona.

I started getting asked to parties by different groups of people. The "cool girls" wanted me to hang out. I noticed that a lot of the kids were drinking, and I thought that was a little crazy.

I had heard that my peers back at my old school in the city were into drugs and alcohol and sex, but I was never actually a part of that scene.

Growing up I had watched my dad get hammered drunk more times than not when he was home. I had also seen both my parents drinking too much with friends and not making good decisions more times than I would have liked.

I was born in Vegas, and my mom jokes that I was born with a cuba libre in one hand and a poker chip in the other. I have never actually gambled, though.

I always said that I would not drink because I had seen what it did to people. I had seen how it affected the decisions that they made. But for some reason, this move was different.

I don't remember the first night that I drank.

But I do know that after I drank, the anxiety I felt around people went away.

I could be more sociable when I drank, and I didn't care as much about what was going on.

Warning Signs

Fast forward many years, and I have come to the realization that I deal with quite a bit of anxiety and depression. I also get overstimulated easily. Looking back, I took on a lot of worries as a child that most kids do not take on. I was sad a lot.

These things were never addressed as issues to be dealt with. Back then, I figured that there was something wrong with me. I struggled a lot with these emotions and drinking at the time helped alleviate those struggles...or so I thought.

I was 14 when I started drinking. I spent several years drinking way too much. I made several bad decisions because of alcohol, and even had run-ins with the law.

You would think that always wanting to do the right thing would have deterred me. My drinking continued anyway.

I was forced to go to an outpatient rehab at the end of my sophomore year of high school.

Needless to say, that did not help. The kids there were all smokers, and one girl even told me she was addicted to sex. This was very uncomfortable for me.

Love, Children, And Alcohol

My junior year of high school I met my "first love". I spent a lot of time with him, and I even moved in with him.

By this point, I thought I had learned how to drink without getting into trouble or getting out of control.

I had only learned to get black out drunk without anyone noticing.

This went on for several years and then I met the man I would have kids with and eventually marry.

I enjoyed having a family of my own. I felt like I was a true adult with a family.

I also felt like a responsible drinker: I only allowed myself to get drunk after my kids fell asleep. But I was still getting drunk. (Note: I did not drink while I was pregnant.)

After our son was born, I noticed that drinking didn't feel the same.

Alcohol was no longer temporarily relieving my anxiety. In fact, my anxiety levels had increased.

I would lie awake almost every night listening closely to the baby monitor to make sure he was breathing. On top of that, my heart would pound and I would sweat due to the alcohol.

I would wake up and feel horrible, almost like I was having "out of body" experiences all the time.

I remember one morning I woke up with my heart pounding. I felt so anxiety-ridden and hungover that I could not take care of my son.

I took him to my dad to watch while I lay in bed and waited for the fears to go away. I knew that something wasn't right, but I had become used to feeling this way.

This went on for another year.

Building The Resolve To Heal

Finally, I decided to put more effort into quitting drinking. I realized that something was not right internally and that I needed to take care of it. I was tired of feeling horrible and losing out on days and precious moments with my son.

I was tired of going on and off of anxiety/depression medication. I had been on these meds since the age of 17, when I had gone to the doctor myself to get them.

Every time I told the doctor that the medication was no longer working, he would prescribe more.

I would always ask him when I could stop taking them. I would get the same answer: "We'll keep you on them and then wean you off eventually." That never happened.

My then-husband and father of my kids received a discount from his employer to an acupuncturist. I did some research and decided to try it.

For awhile, I felt like I was doing well. I was only drinking about every four days, woohoo!

I even got back to the gym and started to lose the baby weight and the alcohol weight.

After a few visits to the acupuncturist, I started sleeping better. My anxiety levels decreased significantly. I also got hooked up with some ladies from church who sold essential oils, which worked well.

A month after I had started my journey toward "getting better", I got pregnant with our daughter. My body was focused on growing a baby, not repairing itself.

After my daughter was born, I quickly got back into drinking.

However, my drinking had significantly decreased. I was hitting the gym more and more, and I was really getting into the essential oils. I had stopped going to the acupuncturist due to time and money, but I was starting to feel much better.

I was still doing research. I started realizing that maybe healing my body naturally was the way to go. I found a good chiropractor in the area who helped me change my life.

Still, I was nervous because I felt that my brain was not working like it should.

Back To Square One

I was still having those strange "out of body" experiences. I was at times unable to hold intelligent conversations, and I would say things that people normally wouldn't say.

I had a meeting scheduled with a neurologist around the same time as the chiropractor. I decided to give the chiropractor a chance before I went through all the testing that the neurologist suggested. It was amazing how much better I started to feel.

My then-husband saw the same chiropractor, and he even quit smoking, something that he was unable to accomplish after so many years.

I was really starting to get going with a more holistic approach to taking care of myself and repairing my body.

Suddenly, things got bad between my then-husband and me. I had to leave him.

We went through a long and ugly divorce. My depression became worse than ever.

I had two little ones to take care of, mostly on my own. I went from being a stay-at-home mom for six years to going into the working world.

My alcohol cravings increased severely. I thought about drinking every day. It seemed like every minute.

When I did not have the kids, I found myself able to go through a bottle of tequila, or 2-3 bottles of wine.

My body started bloating up after drinking. My face would feel swollen. It would take me days to recover.

I would quit, only to start again.

I didn't like who I was when I drank. I didn't make good decisions when I drank. I was supposed to be the one taking care of my kids, and I was having a hard time taking care of myself. I would cry and get angry that I was unable to quit drinking.

Why would I go back when I knew what alcohol did to me?!

Trial And Error

I searched and searched for answers. I tried this, I tried that. I knew that AA or rehab were not the answer since I had tried both of them before.

Then one night, I came across Fit Recovery.

I immediately bought Chris's eBook by the name of "Drinking Sucks." I began to feel really dedicated.

I went over 20 days without drinking, and that was incredible for me.

I was starting to feel better again. I was making strides to do better and to be better.

However, I would take two steps forward and then I would drink again and feel like I was taking three steps back.

I knew that I had so many goals and dreams that I could accomplish if I could just quit drinking!

I had to do this for my kids. Never had I ever wanted something so bad. I needed to quit for my kids. They deserved so much more.

So, why couldn't I quit? Why would I get to the 20-day mark only to fall short?

You would think that when your "Why" is something so important to you that your accomplishment would come easy. That's not the case. It just means that you can go the extra mile to accomplish your goal.

I was willing to stick it out. This wasn't easy. If you can have just one drink, you may not fully understand the chains of alcohol addiction. I was a slave.

But I continued to implement the nutrient repair and recovery process Chris speaks about so often.

I could tell that these things were starting to make me feel better.

I decided to buy Chris's online course. I started taking Chris's recommended supplements and hitting the gym more. Man, that was a turning point!

I also started asking others who have immersed their lives into holistic healing about other supplements and vitamins that would help.

I found out that I was suffering from adrenal fatigue.

This made sense with all of the stress that I had been living with for so long. I started taking a supplement for adrenal health that contains rhodiola extract and holy basil leaf.

Breakthrough: The View From 82 Days!!!

My goal was to be disgusted by alcohol. When I first started Chris's Total Alcohol Recovery course, I watched a video of Chris saying that for him, drinking alcohol would be like drinking paint thinner.

While I may not be disgusted to this extent by alcohol, I am proud to say that I have zero desire to drink it. I do now feel disgusted by the thought of drinking.

At 82 days alcohol-free, I am so excited and happy to be on this journey of self-healing.

Our bodies are so amazing, and it is miraculous to see how quickly they can repair.

When we take care of our bodies, they take care of us.

I do not tell everyone my story, but whoever is suffering from being enslaved to alcohol I tell them that I was there too.

I lead them to Fit Recovery because it has changed my life.

I am now 31, and I have a lot of experience in holistic health research, trial and error, and downright disgust with myself.

All of this in order to finally say that I am happy.

I have gone through hell so that I too can help others going through the same thing, and now I can assure them that I TOO HAVE BEEN THERE!

CHAPTER 16

THE RISE OF FUNCTIONAL MEDICINE

"The doctor of the future will no longer treat the human frame with drugs, but rather will cure and prevent disease with nutrition."
-Thomas Edison

Thanks to the explosion of health-focused websites, podcasts and YouTube channels, personalized health optimization now occupies the spotlight.

This is very good news. Healthcare politics aside, a philosophical reboot of the assumptions underlying our healthcare system is long overdue.

Prescription medications taken correctly kill over 100,000 Americans per year. Millions of Americans die each year from preventable diseases like Type 2 diabetes and heart disease. Many people hospitalized with these conditions die from hospital errors, which in total kill about 500,000 people each year – a population the size of Miami.

Hard-working doctors and nurses cannot be blamed. Too many people take prescription drugs in lieu of altering their lifestyles and ultimately end up in the hospital with preventable chronic diseases. To make matters worse, only a minority of doctors have any training in nutrition or chemical dependency.

Fortunately, disease prevention has entered the popular radar. The idea of waiting until we get sick and then heading to the doctor for a pill seems increasingly wrongheaded.

People with conditions ranging from depression, chronic fatigue, intestinal disorders, and skin rashes have found relief by addressing the underlying causes of their malaise instead of suppressing their symptoms indefinitely with pharmaceutical drugs.

We hear stories about people who eliminate gluten or dairy from their diets, resolving three or four seemingly disparate symptoms at once. For people with certain food sensitivities, excising the offending foods may decrease systemic inflammation, alleviating their symptoms as well as reducing their risk for developing chronic disease. Other people might be advised to correct hormonal imbalances or specific nutrient deficiencies.

This philosophy of health is called Functional Medicine. It blends all of the tools of modern medicine with holistic considerations based on emerging research.

One of the cornerstones of Functional Medicine is the concept of biochemical individuality. In time, we will likely see the development of apps and even Artificial Intelligence systems that synthesize a dizzying array of variables – from genetic factors, to ancestral diet considerations, to local air pollution – to help people optimize their health.

Most importantly, Functional Medicine is helping a new generation of doctors to become re-enchanted with medicine in the first place.

The Health Information Revolution

Hundreds of scientific papers relevant to our health are published every day. A decade ago, it would have been impossible to keep up with this stream of research without consulting a research database and speed-reading all day.

Even then, it would have been difficult to find information

detached from the "pill for an ill" approach to health. Pharmaceutical companies fund medical school research, shape physicians' continuing educations, lobby politicians, and constantly advertise their drugs. They also maintain deep relationships with government agencies like the FDA.

MedLinePlus.gov, the website for The National Library of Medicine, has an odd history of excluding many studies that take a nutritional approach to health. For example, it has been criticized for failing to include in its database many peer-reviewed studies on nutrition by Linus Pauling, the only scientist to win two Nobel Prizes.

With faith in the status quo waning, people have turned to the Internet for fresh information. For any condition you can imagine, you can find multiple websites offering relatable stories and in-depth information. While scrambling eggs in the morning, you can listen to your favorite podcast personality interview pioneers in health research.

Anyone with a smartphone can instantly tune in to segments with epigenetic researchers, longevity scientists, gut health experts, and clinicians specializing in ketogenic diets for mental health disorders.

People with undetected Lyme Disease, hypothyroidism, or chronic pain are often accused of making up their symptoms. Parents of children with ADHD are typically given two options: Adderall or Ritalin. Functional Medicine offers a glimmer of hope for people suffering from chronic health problems.

The Next Domino: Addiction Recovery

I too once struggled for years with a condition that traditional medicine could not fix. Like many other people, I took my health into my own hands.

According to mental health experts, I had a "chronically relapsing spiritual disease" called alcoholism. They said that there was no cure. Detox would treat physical symptoms of withdrawal, but after that, the only known treatment was spiritual.

I later learned that this bleak picture was mostly false. People certainly benefit from spiritual transformation after quitting drinking, but this is far from the only tool at their disposal.

Clinicians have experienced success since the 1950s using infusions of basic vitamins, minerals, and amino acids to significantly reduce relapse rates. In 1968, Dr. Linus Pauling himself coined the term Orthomolecular Medicine, which "aims to restore the optimum environment of the body by correcting imbalances or deficiencies based on individual biochemistry."

This approach should sound familiar to anyone who keeps up with health blogs or podcasts. Supplementation and biochemical individuality are recurring themes that have entered the zeitgeist. Supplementation is a tool of Functional Medicine; biochemical individuality is a principle.

Yet when applied to the realm of addiction recovery, these ideas are far from mainstream. Most doctors either throw up their hands or sneer at them. How could this be the case?

A search on Google for "orthomolecular" returns 725,000 results. The same search on National Library of Medicine returns zero results. The Journal Of Orthomolecular Medicine is peer-reviewed and has been published for nearly half a century. It has been rejected numerous times by The National Library of Medicine for technical reasons such as missing paperwork.

Still, rehab centers with success rates averaging 10% have started paying lip service to terms like "holistic recovery." They seem to be aware of buzzwords without quite understanding the science underlying them. A notable exception is Health Recovery Center in Minnesota, which uses Orthomolecular Medicine and was found in a long-term impact study to boast a 74% average abstinence rate after three years.

Basic supplements and lifestyle changes saved my life despite my initial skepticism. I now see that my years of heavy drinking caused malnutrition that led to biochemical imbalances in my body and brain. The symptoms of these imbalances included anxiety, depression, insomnia, lethargy, and alcohol cravings that might have persisted for the rest of my life.

I have not had a drop of alcohol in over 4 years, nor do I have any desire to drink at all. I have been consistently free from the anxiety, depression, and cravings associated with alcohol addiction. Countless readers of this book have experienced similar results. None of this would have been possible without the inspiration and information I gathered from rising pioneers like Rhonda Patrick, Peter Attia, and Chris Kresser.

Having successfully recovered from alcohol addiction, I now want to optimize my body completely. My next step is to make an appointment with a Functional Medicine provider to test for genetic anomalies and environmental toxins.

We are in the midst of the worst drug and alcohol addiction epidemic in our history. Traditional recovery orthodoxy remains in the Dark Ages. I am not advocating for scientific certainty (an oxymoron) or the replacement of one monolithic system with another. The inclusion of nutrient repair and physiological considerations can help people who already benefit from prescription drugs or spiritual support groups.

The rise of Functional Medicine offers us an opportunity to devise a truly multi-dimensional approach to addiction recovery; one that accounts for new research and biochemical individuality in addressing the underlying causes of disorders that were once written off as "mental" problems.

Despite resistance from the powers that be, the overarching trends in science and health are pointing in the right direction. People who pay attention can now find answers that they might have been missing for years.

CHAPTER 17

HOW I LIVE MY OBSESSION

"The unexamined life is not worth living."
-Socrates

Fit Recovery began as an attempt to motivate people who could relate to the horrors of my heavy-drinking my past. I had no idea that my newfound mission would eventually turn my old "real jobs" into mere stepping stones.

That this ultimately came to pass is still surreal to me. My former careers – mostly in finance, with a brief stint in technology – had seemed like the most important things in the world at the time. I was often reminded that "other people would kill for your job!" I felt guilty for failing to muster the passion that my bosses deserved. While I know that my addiction was a biochemical phenomenon that gave clues long before I entered the workforce, I also believe that my guilt over hating my jobs hastened the pace at which I descended to rock bottom.

In my state of alcohol-fueled delusion, the futility of finding fulfillment at work began to seem like a conspiracy. I lived in a society that apparently wanted me to do mind-numbing work for the rest of my life. After wasting away all day in a cubicle, my social life involved meeting up with friends for drinks, with conversations beginning like this: "So, how's work?" My half-truths in response to this question further drained me.

Now I can see that there was no conspiracy. The only thing that compelled me into jobs I disliked was my own hungover complacency. Even more, the very same "system" that seemed to swallow years of my life also enabled the rise of the Internet, which eventually liberated me (and millions of others) from 9-5 drudgery.

The story of how I built a viable career out of my pursuit of a better recovery is worth discussing for several reasons. It shows that the desire to harness your talents to enrich the lives of others is the key to personal fulfillment. It also highlights the possibility of an independent career path for those of us who fall into the "creative" category. For whatever reason, we seem to find ourselves at a higher risk for sliding into chemical dependency – and for hating traditional jobs.

Yet there is an even deeper reason that I want to share this story. Many problems attributed to "the disease of alcoholism" are by no means confined to ex-drinkers: restlessness and discontent are everywhere, and very few people are happy with their current jobs. According to a recent poll, 70% of Americans feel unfulfilled by their work.

Of course, there is also a physiological component to mass discontent. Walk into any grocery store and observe the sheer amount of sugar-laden, pro-inflammatory, highly processed foods packed into the average cart. Nearly 70% of Americans take prescription medications, with antibiotics, antidepressants, and opioids leading the list.

So much for the so-called "normies." Only a minority of people take care of their bodies and pursue work that excites them. If you're trying to conquer alcohol addiction, it's within your power to frame recovery as an opportunity to get a fresh start in these two areas – health and fulfillment – where the vast majority of people fail.

As for myself, I did not shift into a healthy lifestyle and meaningful career overnight. Before I started Fit Recovery, I left behind a lucrative career in finance to make $25 per hour as a personal trainer. Among my friends, many of whom still wore suits and climbed ladders at big banks, the inside joke was that I might lose my mind, dress up like a clown, and hide out in the woods, in line with bizarre news reports of "clown scares." Pay cuts can be scary.

My friends had a laugh when I actually was paid a piddling amount to be a clown during a children's party at the gym.

As a trainer, I genuinely enjoyed helping people transform their fitness. My work felt meaningful; watching people achieve their physical goals was infinitely more satisfying than crunching numbers. Still, my lofty vision was to help even more people beat alcohol addiction via the Internet. My creative nature yearned for freedom from designated hours in the same old place. I now see the clown ordeal as the universe's attempt to make me laugh during a period in which I often wondered whether I would only feel semi-fulfilled for the rest of my life.

For about two years, I split my time between the gym – training people and rebuilding my body from the ravages of alcohol – and my website, which was my real obsession. I stayed up late, reading dozens of books and hundreds of studies on alcohol addiction. Even though few people were reading my articles, I knew that I had stumbled across life-altering information that mainstream recovery programs were ignoring. I wanted to guide people toward feeling physically better, and in so doing, help them to complete their own spiritual transformations. But how on earth would I find these people?

At several points, I considered giving up on this project completely. The costs of maintaining my website – hosting fees, software purchases, hours spent writing instead of training – were compounded by my obsession. I was spending thousands of dollars on supplements and healthy foods to support my own recovery. I felt great, but I spent a lot of money.

Like many novice bloggers, I had an Amazon affiliate account that allowed me to earn a few cents each time someone bought something that I recommended. After writing over 30 articles, I finally received a check for $11. I was extremely excited and immediately blew the proceeds on an $11 supplement (from Amazon) called DLPA.

While that particular supplement changed my life, $11 every few months was not enough to sustain my efforts. I decided to write my first eBook and I was thrilled to make a sale immediately. I quickly discovered that the buyer was my uncle. I was grateful for his interest, but I wanted to earn my financial freedom from strangers who valued my work.

I began reading books about how to create a successful website and stumbled upon guest posting, in which bloggers offer free articles to other bloggers in similar niches, as a strategy for growing my audience. Writing for other websites created new friendships and led me to a seasoned mentor who infused me with motivation and helped me bring my website to the next level. I could no longer afford to be a hermit writer; real growth requires establishing relationships with other people.

As I continued to read books about the art of attracting readers and writing about topics that interest them, Fit Recovery's growth exploded. I quickly began selling hundreds of copies of my eBook, gained dozens of new private coaching clients, and designed an online course to offer people more depth of information and support. I began to upgrade my website. With my website finally out-earning my personal training job, I quit that gig to focus on my real obsession.

Still, personal training was the first job I ever quit that I actually missed doing. Since it was my first job after quitting drinking, it was my first clear-minded adult endeavor. I had become quite close to many of my clients. After I quit, I turned my living room into a gym – and I still occasionally train some of my favorite former clients when I can find the time. Problem solved!

I do get the occasional email from people who are very upset that I earn money from my books and programs. In one sense, the implication is flattering: that the topics to which I've devoted the past four years of my life are extremely important – so much so that anyone should be entitled to my labor for free. The reality is that if I had failed to turn Fit Recovery into a viable small business, neither my book nor my online course would exist – and I would be working with a client in the gym instead of writing these words.

On the bright side, thousands of people have begun to emulate these recovery methods to build a more fulfilling life. Being transparent about my past and documenting my journey have allowed me to become a role model of sorts. In writing this chapter, my goal is to be transparent about my business so that other "creative types" out there can expand their perception of life's possibilities.

Each of us will have to confront our own personal struggle. If you emerge from your struggle with the ability to convey specialized guidance that other people want, then you have the foundation for a new business. Thanks to modern technology, we live in an unprecedented era of potential freedom.

Your only enemies are procrastination and negativity. Trust me, these are worthy adversaries. But when you live your obsession, you free yourself from work as you've always known it. For myself and many of my private coaching clients, freedom from alcohol ultimately paved the way for freedom from drudgery.

Freedom from drudgery is priceless. The heights to which your vision soars will be limited only by the intensity of your own obsession.

CHAPTER 18

LETTERS & COMMENTS

I started Chris's online course at the end of January, 2018. This course was amazing for me. I still read parts of it and I have had no cravings, even with a serious family split right now. I haven't succumbed. No need. Today is 223 days clean and sober. No alcohol in our house...I feel really good, some anxiety from the family issue, but I know it will go away eventually. So just hang in there, and you will be a winner.

Thank you Chris for all of your messages and feedback. I commend you for such a wonderful program.
Mary Lou 73 years old, and free at last.

I am a 49 yr old male fitting the category of 5-10 drinks a day to 'relieve' the stresses from my business. High functioning alcohol addict is best description.

Lifestyle including nutrition and regular gym training has not been an issue for me, however drinking regularly has been. Result....general tiredness and looking like sh*t, and a growing midline!

I committed to an Australian 'Pause for Cause' program raising money for children, which I have undertaken previously. It is basically quitting something for the (shortest!) month of Feb. For me it's beer.

A little bit of web-search prior led me to Fit Recovery. Fantastic stuff.

Last beer for me was 28th Jan and I have used your techniques, advice and 'warnings' on withdrawal to keep at it. Gotta say, apart from sleeping issues, which are getting better, I am smashing it. Moving forward I will take the no alcohol route past the end of Feb and make a lifestyle change.

My personal trainer and all those around me (that matter) have been mint, with my PT particularly taking me to another level training wise. Amazing how much better I can actually feel in such a short time. I have taken the approach that I don't want to poison my body and will train hard and eat/supplement well moving forward.

I wish to be that bloke that doesn't drink and looks after himself moving forward.

You have supplied me with many tools and a better understanding of our bodies and the effects alcohol has on it.....poison!

Thanks again Chris and all the best to you.

Chris, Perth Western Australia

Hi Chris,

You've been on my mind for some reason and so I thought I would drop you this quick note. I wanted to let you know that I am doing FANTASTIC. I realized this morning that I don't have any PAWS or alcohol cravings, but the best part of all is I don't even think about drinking or alcohol. Once I realized this, I knew that I had passed the point of "no return to drinking ever!" I quit smoking 30 years ago and it was tough, but I remember when I passed the milestone of not dreaming about smoking at night or thinking about it in the daytime. I knew I had been healed. I would no more pick up a cigarette now than I would snort a line of cocaine or heroin (oh yes...I had the joy of having to go to hell and back with "street drugs" too). I can now say that while quitting drinking was one of the hardest tests of all (because I had been doing it SO long) it gives me supreme pleasure to be able to say I am completely drug and alcohol free and I feel better than I have in YEARS!

Thank you again for all of your inspiration in getting me to this point. There are SO MANY of us (I hope) out there that just can't go the AA route and are looking for better / different alternatives such as the ones you provide. Take care Chris!

All the best,

Dusty, Sarasota FL

I've been taking all of the supplements (including CBD oil) every day for the last 8 days. I'm not sure which supplement is curbing my cravings but I don't have the uncontrollable craving right now. I did break open one of the L-glutamines the other day and place it under my tongue as a pre-emptive strike against a liquor store stop on my way home from work. I believe I'm one of those who gets the benefit without really feeling a major difference from any one supplement.

I noticed the Tryptophan doesn't really help me sleep (it may keep me up). I'm almost finished with your video on mental/ psychological strategies for quitting for good. I love the supplements but the cognitive strategies is where I think the battle will be won for me! I really had to reframe the belief that "alcohol relaxes me and I deserve it" - it is probably the last held false belief I had about alcohol that inspired/justified my drinking. Thanks for all of the information Chris!

Charles

I am on day 11 with no alcohol. I've been taking all of the recommended supplements daily, working out and eating well. I am absolutely amazed at how well the supplements are working for me. I feel so much better! My skin is better (my husband even commented on it) my energy level is better! I'm more connected with what's happening with my body. I can't stop talking about these supplements!

I had one mild craving early on, but I took L-Glutamine and got through it. I've been in 2 different situations that would have normally sent me into high anxiety (crowded restaurant with lots of chaos & noise going on, over-stimulus). It didn't even faze me. It's hard to pinpoint the exact feeling to describe, but now it's just easier to go with the flow and let things happen, good or bad. Situations just don't bother me the way they did before, yet I'm fully present in the moment. It's so refreshing.

My son said to me, "Mommy you laugh easier now, and you seem so happy all the time." Although it kills me that he has seen me so unhappy, I am so thankful that I'm making this change for myself and especially my family. I've been very honest with my family about quitting for good, for my health and happiness.

Chris, I want to thank you from the bottom of my heart for this e-course. It has been worth every penny. I've tried to quit before and had horrible withdraws which lead me back to drinking. I now fully understand that what I was experiencing was PAWS. No wonder I didn't make it very long, I was merely using will power to cut out alcohol, yet I had build my life around it. I truly believe that now, thanks to this course, I have the tools and the right plan to quit for good. I'm so hopeful for the future. I feel like a hermit that has finally ventured outside, and it's beautiful. There is so much potential now. Thank you again!

Mykel

I started with reading Fit Recovery, then "Drinking Sucks!" and now enjoying your course. It's been 29 days alcohol free. Taking the supplements and just started exercising too now trying to get up earlier and apply morning techniques. Thanks Chris. I'm learning to come out of the shadows and looking to celebrate my new life with all the blessings I am finding being alcohol free and learning to love myself and others.

Lois

Chris,

Thank you so much for your warm, honest, and encouraging responses. It feels very good to admit my problem and issues to others. Knowing that one is not alone somehow helps.

Thank you so much for your exhaustive research, dedication, experimentation & information with supplementation. But more so, your compassion of sharing your experience and findings on Fit-Recovery.com. I bought your e-book, and your course is the next step. I am very happy for you that this is a labor of love and that you enjoy helping people. All of this has been worth every cent and in my opinion even more.

Bob

Hi Chris,

In advance, I apologize for being extremely wordy in but I just can't seem to say enough!

I just wanted to drop you a line to say THANK YOU from the bottom of my heart for creating Fit Recovery and offering so much undervalued and overlooked advice in regards to quitting drinking.

I stumbled across this blog 4 nights ago around 2 am from yet another seemingly "last ditch effort to help myself not die Google search" whilst in the throes of yet another withdrawal - a drenched in cold sweat, chest pounding, body shaking nightmare. I definitely also have the hallmark trait of obsessive curiosity you described (you know, the one I was constantly reprimanded for in recovery and called "too smart for my own good"), Sorry but I refuse to be a sheeple, people! I read a few of your posts and then immediately purchased your book and read the whole thing that night. When I was finished, I finally felt that "spark" of hope for my recovery that I think I've only felt once before- on the plane ride to my first inpatient treatment stay where I thought I'd finally be "cured" hah.

I have never related to someone's story of addiction as much as I do yours and I think that's why your views on recovery actually make tangible sense to me, I was a very bright kid, hell bent on success in everything I put my mind to. In high school I excelled athletically and academically, graduating with a 98% avg, earning a full scholarship to University. I never once touched alcohol in high school fearing I would become addicted like my dad had been but still went to parties and had a great social life. That being said, I was utterly terrified of failure and had started exhibiting anxious and depressive tendencies.

Throughout University I managed to not only develop a massive alcohol problem but also a severe case of bulimia which is not a fun combo yet is an incredibly common one. I had my first drink in my 3rd year, had that Trojan horse "OMG this is what I've been looking for all my life!" experience, and was drinking morning to night every day by the end of that week. *Brain circuitry unlocked and engaged*.. I did manage to graduate and hold down a job, I still have no idea how I hid my problems from mostly everyone but the addict brain craving its fuel is more devious than I'd like to admit.

The subsequent years til' now in a nutshell include lots of alcohol, food, failed relationships, hospitalizations, detox facilities, psychiatrists, cross-country moves trying to escape from my problems, more $$$ wasted than I even want to think about. There were two stays in treatment- The first was 3.5 months and almost $40,000 where everything was A.A. based, minimal treatment for my ED. NO nutritional therapy or exercise (gee, ya think maybe I might have been a little malnourished?) Then sent to a recovery house where I was kicked out for engaging in my ED. A few months later in

MUCH worse shape I was hospitalized and sanctioned to detox where I nearly died from acute kidney failure. I had ataxia and couldn't walk in a straight line, couldn't form sentences. Went back to treatment for a month for a $15,000 stabilization period (which felt more like a shame-based *let's look at how many ways you didn't follow your AA program* session). They released me to a sober house on the opposite side of the country from my family where I lived for 7 months (with SIX other sick women on the top floor of a house) with mandatory AA meetings every night. I felt more depressed and anxious than ever yet had been abstinent from my ED since treatment (out of pure self-will, not their help). When I was released I was also still on massive amounts of valium and the taper process was hell on earth. I stayed sober for almost 2 years and those years were only mildly better than being dead.

I had PAWS like crazy and was told to pray it away or work my program harder like I wasn't trying hard enough. It was recommended I stay on the opposite side of the country from my family and friends to remove any temptations. I did everything I was supposed to do to feel better and still felt terrible. The anhedonia was killing me and trying to find motivation to do anything was impossible. I flip flopped between being suicidal and being so anxious I couldn't move I was shaking so badly. I couldn't wait for the fateful day   I could drink again to feel some sort of relief. So back in June I started drinking again and it was okay for a short bit until it definitely wasn't okay. And then it was way worse and then I was "sick of being sick" (<I felt this post needed a cliche for some reason).

And to think that in three days of taking a high quality multivitamin, magnesium, l-glutamine, and chamomile (all I've been able to get so far) I honestly feel better than I have in 10 years is borderline miraculous. It was almost IMMEDIATE relief from the internal shaking, tremors, brain fog, and anxiety, I couldn't believe it. I also didn't experience any further withdrawals which I count as just being graced this one last time. I believe it was an extreme magnesium deficiency in recovery that in my YEARS of seeking help no one thought to mention. I currently have very minimal cravings for alcohol and when I do, I take some l-glutamine and they go away within 10 minutes.

I am in AWE. It feels like a miracle. I was in tears reading your book because I finally feel for the first time that not only is long-term sobriety possible for the *difficult to treat*, but that it can be rewarding and not an eternal prison of misery, self-doubt, and dogma. I look forward to it being an exciting opportunity for renewed growth and becoming the woman I know I am capable of being.

THANK YOU SO MUCH for helping me!

Marie

ABOUT CHRIS SCOTT

I hope that in these pages, you have found information that will help you leave drinking in the past and become the person you were meant to be.

To learn more about me and the ideas presented in this book, please visit **Fit-Recovery.com**. (Don't forget the dash!) You can subscribe to my email list for free, and you'll find a ton of free information on my website.

I recommend specific products on my website - supplement brands that have worked for me, books and studies that helped me to understand addiction, even the light box I use on rainy days.

Let's connect on social media!

> **Facebook: /FitAndRecovered**
> **Twitter: @FitAndRecovered**
> **Instagram: @ChrisScottFR**

I ask only one thing of you: If you know anyone who might be helped by this book, please recommend it to them!

Thank you, dear reader, for purchasing my book.

Chris Scott

Made in the USA
Middletown, DE
27 January 2019